FROM STEEL TOES TO STILETTOS

Give a Girl the Right Pair of Shoes & She Can Conquer the World

RaNae Envy

and

co-authored with **Raymond Aaron**

AuthoritiesPress

Publisher 10-10-10 Publishing Markham, ON Canada

DEDICATION

THIS BOOK IS DEDICATED TO the loving memory of my mother, Linda Carol Hughes and my grandmother, Leoda Hughes. You have finished the race, and now wear the crown.

Also, to all the women that are the strongest among us and are the true architects of the future and the soul.

TABLE OF CONTENTS

Acknowledgements ix

Foreword xi

Introduction **Well-Behaved Women Seldom Make History** 1

                Iron Lady 5

Chapter 1 **"Death Is Not the Greatest Loss in Life. The Greatest Loss Is What Dies Inside Us While We Live."** 9

                A Snake in the Grass 12

                Barfly 13

                It's A Wonderful Life 14

                Dead Poet's Society 16

                One Flew Over the Cuckoo's Nest 17

                The Impossible 18

Chapter 2   **"They Tried to Bury Us, But They Didn't Know That We Were Seeds."** **21**

The Choice 23

Betrayed 26

Suck It Up, Buttercup 28

Edge of Tomorrow 32

Unbreakable 36

Chapter 3   **Give a Girl the Right Shoes and She Can Conquer the World** **43**

The Pursuit of Happiness............................49

Starting Point 56

Superman 60

Chapter 4   **The Airplane Takes Off Against The Wind, Not With It.**....................................**63**

Soul Surfer...66

Against All Odds..69

Inner Issues...70

External Issues...73

Miracle 74

Chapter 5   **Ours Is Not To Reason Why, Ours Is But To Do or Die** **75**

We Are Marshall 81

Places Of The Heart 82

Feelings..84

Unbroken 86

The Finishers 88

Chapter 6   **She Lives a Life She Didn't Choose and It Hurts Like a Pair of New Shoes 91**

Carrie 96

Patch Adams 105

The Usual Suspects 106

Against All Odds Again 108

Chapter 7   **You Don't Have To Be Great To Start, But You Have To Start To Be Great.........111**

Reality Bites 113

Facing The Giants 115

My Story 119

Floating 121

Chapter 8   **All That I Am, Or Hope To Be, I Owe To My Angel Mother. 123**

Suicide Squad 127

Inception 128

The Secret Garden 132

Chapter 9   **Injustice Anywhere Is A Threat To Justice Everywhere.............................137**

Bruce Almighty 140

Infinity War 142

Doctor Who 146

*Alice in Wonderland: Through
the Looking Glass* 146

You Are The One With The Power 149

On The Basis of Sex 150

Chapter 10   **NO Excuses on the Road to Success!** **153**

*The Secret of My Success—5 Principles
To Live By* 162

Chapter 11   **A Star Is Born** **167**

Tucker: The Man and His Dream 169

On Your Mark, Get Set 176

Chapter 12   **If They Don't Give You A Seat At
The Table, Bring A Folding Chair** **177**

Change Your Life 180

It Is Time 182

ACKNOWLEDGEMENTS

WOULD LIKE TO GIVE MY highest gratitude to the following people: Raymond Aaron, Jennifer Varga-Auten, Jacque Mancuso, Mary Sigwart-Hollingshead, Leah Wall, Cathleen Carpenter, Lisa Meador-Cassese, Shadia Rasul, Sarah Kahler, Justin Ulrich, Gerald Ulrich, Clarissa Hughes, Kyle Ulrich, and Janine Chmielewski.

Also to Chad Watson, Frances Chau, Alexander Rode, Jennifer Hechko-Meyers, Tiffany Lowther, Linda Gillan, Ken Walls, Mary Romero, Kim Thompson-Pinder and Michala Lowther who supported me at every turn and without whom it was impossible to accomplish the end task.

FOREWORD

I APPLAUD RaNae Envy's courage in sharing such a powerful story of being able to overcome such adverse circumstances. Instead of allowing these situations to drag her down she rose above and grew stronger through them.

If you have struggled in life, then *From Steel Toes to Stilettos* is the book for you. In it RaNae not only tells you her story but tells you how she overcame abuse, trying to make it in a man's world and the stigma of suicide and mental illness experienced by her mother and Grandfather.

She also shares with you the power of becoming an entrepreneur and how owning her business has changed her life.

One of the most powerful lessons she shares is how to overcome the injustices still occurring today. Women still have far to go in the equality race, and RaNae has experienced it first hand having worked for many years in the male-dominated auto industry and proved that it doesn't matter who you are, it is what you do with what you have that matters.

I highly encourage you to not only read RaNae's book but take action on it. If you are allowing negative circumstances to control your life, then learn from her example and change them to opportunities for growth.

The only time you have is NOW, and one of the best mindsets you can have is to learn from those who have overcome and then do what they did and be victorious yourself.

This book will change how you see adversity. If RaNae can go from steel toes to stilettos, then there is nothing that can stop you from reaching for the stars.

Read this book from front to back and then pick one action that you are going to take to move forward in your life. Changing your life starts with that first step.

—Loral Langemeier
  The Millionaire Maker

INTRODUCTION

"Well-Behaved Women Seldom Make History."

—*Laurel Thatcher Ulrich*

D O YOU DREAM OF YOUR life being more than what it is? Are there desires in your heart that you need to fulfill? Do you long to become the person that you were meant to be?

Join the club that includes almost every person on this planet. We are born with this inner knowing that we were created for greatness. Look at any toddler who struts her stuff and wants the world to know that she is there. That little one knows that she has something to give. Then life happens and the messages that become your inner truth begin.

"You can't do that, you are a girl. Why even bother trying, you are only going to get married and have kids anyways. You were not born to succeed but to be average. Success is hard." All these messages become the subconscious dialogue that rules your life. You know it shouldn't be that way, so you fight it. It is hard when you know that there is more, yet something seems to be holding you back.

Throughout this book I am going to share with you my life and the lessons that have brought me to success. Let me share the first one with you here. What goes on in the three pounds of grey matter between your ears, both consciously and unconsciously, is what determines how far you get in life.

Every single one of us has an angel on one shoulder and the devil on the other. Which one wins? The one you allow to speak into your ear. Words can either speak/breathe life into us or lead us to a slow painful death. You are the gatekeeper to your mind and what you allow to enter your mind builds your subconscious belief.

Our minds are naturally in a negative state. It is up to us to plant the seeds of greatness through our thoughts and hearts. The same is true when working on a garden. The natural state of a garden is weeds. It is up to you to cultivate the raw material, find the weeds, and vigorously and unapologetically pull them out.

There is a story of a man complimenting another on his garden. The man said to the other, "What an abundant and beautiful garden the Lord has blessed you with!" To which the garden owner responded, "Thanks, you should have seen it when he gave it to me." Faith without work is dead!

Plant seeds of greatness and what you grow will amaze you. Whatever you plant will grow more than you imagine. A 100-foot tree can grow from the tiniest of seeds.

Our Creator created you for greatness, yet most people are shrinking. They let the weeds take over in their lives and kill their hopes and dreams. Without hope and dreams, people perish. Don't let that be you.

Are you using your time to deny your greatness or preparing for it?

"Watch your thoughts for they become words.
Watch your words for they become actions.
Watch your actions for they become habits.
Watch your habits for they become your character.
And watch your character for it becomes your destiny.
What we think, we become.
My father always said that . . . and I think I am fine."

—*Margaret Thatcher*

(The first EVER, female British Prime Minister. In addition, she was the longest ever serving British Prime Minister of the 20th century.)

Iron Lady

Iron sharpens iron. When you break the chain for one (yourself), you break the chain for many, and possibly to infinity, so that no other man or woman will have to go through that ever again!

I love Margaret Thatcher. She is the epitome of a strong woman who knew what she wanted, went for it, and never apologized for it. Mrs. Thatcher was a strong believer that your thoughts determine your future.

Check this clip from the movie Iron Lady on the topic of what you think is what you become. https://www.youtube.com/watch?reload=9&v=YZ8CPVa3q0M

Only you can determine your future. No one else gets to make that choice for you. During my childhood and into early adulthood, I was told who I should be and what I should do. As I share my story in this book, you will see that I experienced a very tough world. I did what others told me to do and I was miserable. Not anymore!

Now I choose the life I want to live. Everyday brings me closer to my next goal and dreams. I have accomplished things I never thought possible. Now it is your turn.

"I am asking for a day of Heaven on Earth for me and everyone I come in contact with."

—Maureen J. St. Germain

Read this book with an open mind and allow yourself to dream again. It is time for you to become the person that you have always wanted to be. It is your job to do God's work, because here on Earth, God's/Creator's work must truly be our own. God/Creator never once made a table or chair. He only made a tree, but He gave mankind the ability to create all things through Him!

Before you turn the page and get started, remember the words of Maya Angelou.

"Your crown has already been bought and paid for. Put it on your head and wear it."

Are you ready? Let's go . . .

CHAPTER 1

"Death Is Not the Greatest Loss in Life. The Greatest Loss Is What Dies Inside Us While We Live."

—Norman Cousins

HAVE YOU EVER PLAYED WITH a set of kinetic, balance balls, known as a Newton's Cradle? A wonderful office toy with the balls on the string that you put on your desk. When you see it, you can't resist pulling that one ball back and then letting it go to whack the others, creating a never-ending back and forth. That is what my childhood felt like. A constant back and forth between my parents, with me in the middle, constantly being mentally and emotionally smacked by the two of them.

On one side, my alcoholic/playboy Dad was constantly pushing me to do things way beyond what I was ready for and to be something I wasn't. On the other side, my mentally ill Mom was so filled with fear that she didn't want to do or try anything because something bad might happen.

Can you imagine what life is like when one person is pushing you to do something and the other one is clinging to you trying to get you to stop? Who do you choose when you are a child, and these are the two people you love most in the world? YOU CAN'T CHOOSE! Yet, you are forced to do so constantly. Due to that reality, I took the brunt of displeasure from both. It is a position no child should ever be in, and yet, that is how I grew up. It is something that I'm grateful for because it allowed me to become an independent thinker.

A Snake in the Grass

I am always amazed when you open yourself up to receive good things in life and they find you. Just recently, a good friend of the family from my childhood found me on Facebook as I prepared to start writing this book. She shared some memories of my Mom that I had forgotten. It was incredible because I had wondered how I was going to explain what I went through with my Mom. She gave me the perfect words and story to share.

Now I must warn you! If you are afraid of snakes, please whatever you do, don't picture in your mind what is happening as you read this story. It might freak you out!

I was five years old, standing outside our house with my Mom's friend. My mom started to go outside and realized that there was a snake in the yard. She shut the door, overcome by fear, and was going to stay in the house all day, even if it meant ruining the day for all of us. Have you ever had that reaction to snakes? I know in that moment, I was very afraid, and wished I could be in the house.

Then the most awe-inspiring thing happened. The family friend, without an ounce of fear, picked up that snake in the backyard and swung it around her head like a lasso that reached all the way to the front yard. Then she threw it far from the house. The neighborhood kids were outside watching too. It seemed as if Wonder Woman had come to life and was real! She was a true HERO in my eyes!

As I watched her, I wasn't afraid anymore. For those few brief minutes, courage swelled up in my young heart. I knew there was more to life than fear. It was a seed planted in my heart that would stay hidden for many years. When it finally started to grow, there was no stopping it. However, I am getting ahead of myself.

The family friend hit the nail on the head when she described my Mom as having wasted much of her life hiding in fear. When you live like that, then there comes a point where there isn't much to value in your life anymore. She didn't take care of her mind, body, and spirit. In the end, that fear destroyed her.

Barfly

My father was a very hard man to live with. Alcohol was his constant companion! I hated the way it made my Dad act. ::You never knew when he would hit that point where the drink took over and the rage inside him would be released. It wasn't unusual for cars to end up in the ditch when he was driving drunk, but one incident in particular stands out in my mind.

He came home all mad because the car had 'mysteriously' ended up in the ditch again after he had been visiting the bars. My mom and I could tell that he was three sheets to the wind, so when he asked for the keys to the other car to pull the first one out, my mother said no. Instead, she tried to keep the keys from him. At one point, she gave them to me, and I didn't know what to do. Should I run? I looked at my mom and I know she was trying to communicate something to me through her eyes, but at that youthful age, I just couldn't make it out. As my dad grabbed me, I saw the disappointment in her eyes.

When he took the keys out of my hand, there was a great amount of pain but it wasn't physical, although sometimes I almost wish it was. The pain I felt was of defeat and knowing that there was nothing I could do to stop him from bringing chaos home. Parents are supposed to protect their children from terrible things, but what is a child to do when you love the monster that is hurting your family? I carried that feeling in my heart well into adulthood. Thankfully, I don't carry that anymore!

It's A Wonderful Life

At age eleven, my parents divorced. It was unusual. None of my friend's parents were divorced and I wasn't sure what to expect. For a while, I was sure I would end up in an orphanage because that is where kids with no parents went. No one I knew ever had gotten a divorce up to that point. It was a very difficult time in my life and my father wasn't handling it well.

The day we went to the lawyer's office for Mom to sign the papers was particularly bad. My dad was in the parking lot, acting like he was going to run me, my mom, and my younger brother Kyle over as we walked from the office to our car. I was so afraid that day.

It feels as if most memories of my dad are hard and stern, but occasionally, something good would happen. There was one Christmas, not long after the separation, that Dad came over and watched *It's A Wonderful Life* with me. To this day, I can't watch the movie without remembering what happened next.

It was one of the few times that I felt truly loved by my dad. As the movie ended, I looked over at him and he was crying! He never cried, but in that moment, I knew that he cared more than he ever showed about me and our family. It lasted only a fleeting moment and then he got ready to leave. As he hopped into his car, I watched from the window. As the snow was coming down, he struggled to get it to start.

I knew in my heart that I didn't want him to go, so I ran into my mother's room and pleaded with my mom to let him stay. She finally said okay, and I ran to window to wave him down and let him know to come back in. By that time, he had gotten the car started and was backing down the driveway in his red Escort station wagon. I was so sad because I desperately wanted to hold onto that moment where I knew that I mattered to my dad. Now it was gone!

Dead Poet's Society

My grandfather loved me! As the first-born grandchild, I spent a lot of time with him and Grandma. Actually, I spent every weekend with them. Grandpa would come and get me on Friday, and I would stay until well into Sunday afternoon. My grandpa was a Southern Baptist Minister, so every Sunday was the same. We went to church and then to Bob Evans to eat. It was a wonderful break from home, and I looked forward to every single Friday.

Dad would spend most of his weekend in the bars drinking and cheating on Mom. I never knew what Mom did during those times.

Then the worst moment of my life came. When I was eight years old, my grandfather committed suicide, although at the time, I only knew that he had died.

Do you ever wish that there was just one moment in time that you could go back and change? If God allowed it, I know which one I would choose. It would be saying goodbye to my grandpa on the day he died and telling him that I loved him.

It was a normal Sunday and I was getting ready to go home. I wanted to tell Grandpa goodbye, but Grandma said he was sleeping and talked me out of it. Something inside me told me I should, but I obeyed my grandma. A few hours later, he was gone.

We got the phone call in the middle of the night. The house phone woke all of us up. I sat on the couch as my dad answered the phone. When he heard the news. Dad started to scream at my Mom, "Your whole family is (bleeping) nuts. Your whole family is (bleeping) nuts." When I asked what was going on, all I was told was that Grandpa had died. Later I overheard a conversation that he had left a note and I asked about it. That was how I learned he committed suicide.

To this day, I wonder if I had been allowed to say goodbye and tell my grandpa how much I loved him, would he have taken his life that night? Maybe my words would have kept him with us longer. I carried that guilt with me for so long. I know that my grandpa would not want me spending the rest of my life carrying that, so I have chosen to let it go.

One Flew Over the Cuckoo's Nest

The day that my grandfather died, so did my mom. She didn't physically, but mentally, emotionally, and spiritually she did. Mom told my aunt that the suicide made her feel like everything she was told in life was a lie.

My baby brother was only two to three weeks old when Grandpa died. Between the post-partum depression, the guilt my mother felt over Kyle (he almost died when he was born because the umbilical cord was wrapped around his neck three times), and the suicide of her father, Mom went into a mental downward spiral that ended tragically. That period changed my life forever.

National Suicide Prevention Lifeline
Call 1-800-273-8255
Available 24 hours everyday

Mom ended up spending a month away in a mental health unit of a local hospital. When she came home, Mom was not the same. Something in her had snapped. She was GONE . . . and I could no longer trust my mother.

I want you to know that I love my mother very much, but it had to be a strong love that would also protect me too.

The day she came home, Mom started telling me some pretty horrible things that in my young mind I could not believe. My grandma had been watching me and my brother while Mom was away. When she heard what my mom said, Grandma yanked me out of the room and privately said to me, whispering to make sure Mom couldn't hear, "Your Mom is sick. You can't believe anything that she says. She doesn't know the truth anymore. She doesn't know what she is saying!"

The Impossible

After all this sadness, I want you to know that the story has a happy ending. It seems impossible after everything I have gone through in my life, but I have learned how to overcome the pain of my past and live for a better future. That is what this book is about. My journey from the rough life of steel-toed boots to the glamour of stilettos and I invite you to join me.

As I share my journey with you, as I open my heart and let you see inside, I want you to find hope. I want you to see the steps I took and how opportunities opened for me to live a good life. If even one thing I have written helps you, then I know that it was worth everything I went through. If by learning from my pain, it spares you pain, then I will be happy.

So, turn the page and see what happens next. I promise that you will be surprised!

CHAPTER 2

"They Tried to Bury Us, But They Didn't Know That We Were Seeds."

—Dino Christianopoulos

HAVE YOU EVER HEARD THE saying, "Trapped between a rock and a hard place?" That was what my childhood was like. Trapped between two parents. One who loved me, but lived her life in fear and mental illness, and tried to drag me down with her. The other was an alcoholic, selfish playboy who only cared that I did what HE wanted.

BUT . . .

That was nothing compared to the hell and life experiences I faced when I was 20. Yes, I can truly say 'hell.' For most of those days, I faced its fires working in the foundry of a car manufacturing plant. A newspaper ran an article on the plant where they called it "hell's personal bakery" and that is what the plant was for me on many days.

The Choice

Picture it. I'm 20 years old. For the first time in my life, I am in control. After leaving high school, I worked hard and received my real estate license. I was eager to get going on my chosen career. Things were looking bright, but it wasn't long before I realized that it took more than schooling to be successful. You need to develop a network as well. It didn't matter to me at the time because I was finally starting to embrace my freedom and a new direction.

That all changed the day my dad asked me to come over to his place. When I got there, he told me that the car manufacturing company he worked for was hiring and he was going to put my name in. He doesn't ask me if I want him to do this or even if I want to work there. Instead, he just assumes that he knows what is best.

I told him that I didn't want to work there. I didn't want to be dirty all the time. I wanted to be a girl. His response was typical of how he treated me all of my life. "Listen, I am putting your name in. They're only picking 400 names out of 5000. Your name is not even going to be picked, but I am putting your name in anyway." There was no fighting him, so I filled out the forms and he submitted them.

Months went by without hearing anything and I thought that was it. When my dad called to talk to me, I thought nothing about it until I heard those fateful words come out of his mouth. "Hey, I got to tell you something. Your name got picked. You got the job at my company."

At that moment, I felt so defeated and afraid, like someone had taken the air out of my tire. "No! Dad, you said they weren't going to pick my name. I don't wanna work there."

It wasn't even based on my skills, but on a lottery. Each employee got one piece of paper to put a name in. Of course, my dad put my name in. I was his only child old enough to apply.

"Listen, 25 or 30 years and you are out. You are going to make at least $60,000 a year to start. How many of your friends are making that at 20 years old? You are going to have vacations, a pension, full health care (you don't have that in real estate), and a discount on a car. The benefits are unlimited. They'll pay for your college, . . . You don't want to miss this opportunity!"

Even though everything in me said that I should say no, that this wasn't a good decision, I couldn't go against my Father's wishes. "Alright Dad." I knew that I didn't want to do this, but I couldn't argue with the potential money, which was a lot more than what I was making at that time. So, I made 'the choice' and took the job with the company.

I was a third-generation employee, at the same company on the same Cleveland site. My father, three of his brothers, and their father (my grandfather), all had made a good living working for this company and were proud of it. Only there was a DRAMATIC difference . . . I was a GIRL! My experience there was more different than they could imagine.

I often wondered what would have happened if I would have stood up to my German-Italian father, who expected me to be his good 'Little Princess'. His obedient soldier who did everything he wanted—even if it wasn't what was best for me. What would have happened if I told him, "NO, I am not doing that!" But at

20, I wasn't strong enough—YET. I was still trapped, and I felt like these words from Christina Perri's song *Human*:

I CAN FAKE A SMILE
I CAN FORCE A LAUGH
I CAN DANCE AND PLAY THE PART

I CAN DO IT

BUT I'M ONLY HUMAN
AND I BLEED WHEN I FALL DOWN

AND I CRASH AND I BREAK DOWN
YOUR WORDS IN MY HEAD, KNIVES IN MY HEART
YOU BUILD ME UP AND THEN I FALL APART
'CAUSE I'M ONLY HUMAN, YEAH
BE A GOOD MACHINE
I CAN HOLD THE WEIGHT OF WORLDS

The time will come when that will change. For right now, it's off to orientation I go and to a job that would torture me, yet strengthen me to become the woman I was meant to grow into.

Betrayed

There was a two week in-class orientation. It wasn't too bad, as we learned about cars, their parts, and how to take apart and put together an engine. I didn't find the classes too hard because of the things my dad had taught me. My whole life I had helped him work on cars and motorcycles at home. He was always working on something. There were motorcycle engines on the kitchen table far more than there was ever a "real" dinner.

Towards the end of the second week of orientation, we had to tell them where we would prefer to work. There were four different plants on the same company property, which we could end up working in. I called my dad and he told me to write down Engine Plant One or Engine Plant Two because the work is easier, there is air conditioning, and it's a cleaner plant. That is what I did.

On the last day of orientation, I got the shock of my life. I was assigned to the Foundry. I couldn't believe it. Not only did I not get my preferred work, but I got the absolute bottom of the barrel, the worst place to work. As we took the tour of where we were to report on Monday, I saw the fires! A train system on the ceiling moved huge barrels filled with molten iron that were poured out in cascading showers of sparks. The noise was deafening. A constant metal thunder rolled and clanged throughout the foundry. The heat was a relentless barrier. I felt like I was being drawn into hell against my will.

I was very upset when I left. I went straight to my father's house crying.

"What's the matter?"

"We got our assignments today."

"Oh no, you didn't get the foundry, did ya?"

"Yeah, I got the foundry."

"Wait, wait, wait. The foundry is not that bad. As long as you didn't get the cleaning room, there's good parts to the foundry too. So long as you didn't get the cleaning room. The cleaning room is the hardest."

I just started crying because, of course, I had been assigned to the cleaning room. He just looked at me and said, "Oh shit!!!! Listen, you go in there and you put in your time. I will try to use as many connections as I can to get you out of there and get you into the engine plant, but you have to go. You have to do your time. At least get your 90 days in and then they can't mess with you because you will be in the union."

In that moment, I felt so betrayed. Here was the man who was supposed to love and protect me, pushing me into what I felt was hell on earth. There was no compassion, no kindness, and no caring. All my dad thought about was the money and it didn't matter what happened to me. What choice did I have? At that point, I felt like there was nothing I could do but give in and start working there.

Suck It Up, Buttercup

I'm a beautiful young woman working with a bunch of men. Not trying to boast but it is important to my story, because my interactions with them did not always go well. For instance, this one Arabic guy started bringing me coffee on the line. It was nice at first but that quickly turned to aggression and control. He kept telling me that I had to work overtime with him and go out with him. I told him I was with someone already, but he wouldn't take no for an answer.

The first few weeks I worked there, I would leave to go home and have a flat tire. When I went into the plant, he and his cousin would flick their lit cigarettes at me. I felt humiliated but I was helpless to do anything about it. Every day I was afraid and hoped that nothing worse would happen to me. Little did I know that later my life would be in danger.

On top of that, the physical work was so hard that by the time that the shift ended, I could barely move my hands enough to put my car into reverse. My poor fingers were so beat up. While sleeping at night, my hands would form a fist so tight that I couldn't open them in the morning when I woke up. I would have to soak my hands in hot water to just try and get them back.

Every week, my dad would call me and say, "You're not gonna quit, are you? You're not gonna quit."

"No, Dad, I'm not gonna quit."

So, I did the most rational thing I could think of at the time. Before my 90 days were up, I went and bought myself a brand-new Lincoln LS that no one had. Black on Black with heated seats, it had things I didn't even know that cars had. I had to have that prize to put myself through hell every day.

Being on constant afternoons and the very hard work, which was piled on me because I was low (wo)man on the totem pole, was having a negative effect on my life. I would talk to my father and uncle about it and they would say, "Suck it up, Buttercup." There wasn't any compassion for me, because they already had gone through all of it. My uncle would say, "I spent 17 years on afternoons, and I survived."

There is only so much you can take. I eventually got to the engine plants, but over time, did two more tours of the foundry. The last tour was the longest and the hardest.

I wasn't the only one affected by my time in the foundry. Working there at first felt soul-crushing. Despair would worm its way into all parts of your life.

I remember feeling like Alice in Wonderland on multiple occasions.

"But I don't want to go among mad people,"
Alice remarked.
"Oh, you can't help that," said the Cheshire Cat:
"we're all mad here. I'm mad. You're mad."
"How do you know I'm mad?" said Alice.
"You must be," said the Cat,
"or you wouldn't have come here."

—Lewis Carroll, Alice in Wonderland

The four plants were like its own city. You could almost live there and never have to go home. There were some that never did. A few were known for never going home, and the stories were intriguing. One guy named Mo for sure lived in the locker room.

We had locker rooms with showers. Cafeterias for breakfast, lunch and dinner. Our own on campus gym with workout classes. A nurse's station with a nurse around the clock. Our own company doctor kept normal hours and could treat you for anything from the common cold to getting a metal chip out of your eye, which happened often. We had direct deposit and ATM machines in the cafeteria.

It was like a little ghetto that chewed you up and spit you out. One man shot himself and his wife. Another man shot up cars after work. A third man strangled his wife to death during kinky sex.

On top of these stories were my own negative experiences with my co-workers. One guy decided that he didn't like me. He regularly tried to run me off the highway in the middle of the night when there was no traffic, and no one would see him. I endured things like this on a regular basis and yet I said nothing. Who could I tell? My dad wouldn't protect me.

My mother would say to me, "RaNae, RaNae, why do you work so hard? RaNae, why don't you quit that job? That is a man's job. Why don't you get a 'pretty girl' job?"

Now, you may think that she meant it like I wasn't strong enough, but what she really meant was, "You're my beautiful daughter and you don't deserve this hard life." I would say, "Mom, pretty girls don't make no money. If you want to make money, you have to work hard like a man." At the time, I believed it, but now I know better.

I thought my mom told me this because she was poor and broke. She had given up on life and given up on herself. On the other side, my father would say, "Be tall! Be strong. Suck it up, Buttercup!" I was in the middle wondering, "What about me? What about my dreams? What am I meant to do in my life?"

Edge of Tomorrow

I love to look for hope in all things and all circumstances. I even found it in the foundry! There was a lady who worked there who had to throw 75 lbs. side cores (molds) from one palette to the next. She always did it with her make up all done and lipstick on. I knew if she could make it, so could I. I never even spoke to her, but just seeing her being and looking like a woman with dignity and strength was enough to inspire me to be strong too.

I reached a point, eight years in, where I started looking for other opportunities. The car company offered college money for employees interested in pursuing their education. For a brief time, I worked and went to college part-time to study Interior Designer and Marketing. I really enjoyed the classes and got great grades. Soon I realized that with the seniority I had earned at work, it would take forever for my new career to even come close to the salary I was currently earning at the plant. Not to mention the time I would have to invest to make it happen, which meant an extended period of long hours and little income.

Financially it didn't make sense. I would have had to go to college part-time and work full-time, for what, 4-8 years? Only to graduate and start out making half of what the auto industry paid. The other option was to work overtime hours and make more money than even some doctors.

So that is what I did. Instead of registering for another quarter of college, I applied for an internal job as a Fork Lift Driver and started to work as much overtime as I could. I would work afternoons from 4pm-2:30 am and then I'd wash up in the ladies' room and go out to my truck in the parking lot and sleep until 5:30 am and do a split shift of 4 hours until 10am a lot. My mother would call and plead with me, "RaNae, why are you working so much and sleeping in your truck?" I'd tell her, "Mom, I'm making A LOT of money and people who are fighting in wars have to deal with way worse conditions. She would say, "But RaNae, you are not in a war!" That period was the first time I made over $100,000 in my life. Wow! I did it! I got to 6 figures!

That was the most money any woman in my family had ever made. Heck, it was more money than my brother had ever made.

Still, college had benefits. My college time was a wonderful experience that showed me that I had more to offer to the world.

In addition to working at the plant, I had another business venture of flipping houses with my dad, but that wasn't getting me anywhere. Basically, I was doing a good portion of the work and he never gave me a single penny. Due to my real estate background, I would know exactly what to buy, go to the auction, buy the house, help Dad fix it up, and I never got anything. It was all his money. It taught me that any true wealth I wanted to acquire, I would have to do it myself. I would not get any help.

It wasn't long until I went to the auction by myself with my own checkbook and bought my first home. A complete fixer-upper that needed everything, but it was MINE! My little bit of earth. My father helped me with a lot of the fixing up, especially the painting.

Then came the 2008 financial crisis. The crash of September 2008 brought the largest bankruptcies in world history, pushing more than 30 million people into unemployment and bringing many countries to the edge of insolvency.

The Big Three automakers asked <u>Congress</u> for help similar to the <u>bank bailout</u>. They warned that General Motors Company and Chrysler LLC faced bankruptcy and the loss of 1 million jobs.

Ford Motor Company didn't take any bailout funds because it had already cut costs, through wage and benefit decreases agreed to by the employees to keep their jobs and by mortgaged their entire brand. However, Ford asked to be included so it wouldn't suffer the plight of a complete shuttered industry. The Big Three shared many of the same part suppliers, so to let 2 of the 3 go down would affect the cost of doing everyday business, let alone survival in the unforeseen future.

"All you can do, is all you can do!"

—Art Williams

With all the uncertainty surrounding our future, the plant was filled with fear. Everyone was talking about what we were going to do next.

It also happened to be a Presidential Election year in the United States. Barack Obama was running for president and I volunteered to work on his campaign. The Democratic Committee was so impressed with me that they chose me to give a speech and introduce Hillary Clinton when she came to Ohio on behalf of Obama. They wanted a hard-working American woman to discuss how everyday American workers were suffering and falling further and further behind.

What an incredible opportunity! I was so scared that I couldn't sit still. I had constant butterflies in my stomach. How was I going to do this? I was being stretched well beyond my comfort zone. At a time when a little support and encouragement would have gone a long way, neither of my parents came to see me speak. Mom was too sick, and Dad was away at one of his out of state homes. I was deeply disappointed.

However, my aunt came with me. She knew that I could do this and more. At one point, when my nerves were getting the better of me, I stated to her, "I don't think I can do this!" She smiled and said, "If I didn't think you could do this, I wouldn't be here!"

The lesson I learned in that moment is that sometimes you must 'borrow' someone else's belief in you until you can believe in yourself. When you believe in someone else, you give them power. Never underestimate what a few small words or a simple action can do for someone who is struggling.

Halfway into my speech, I looked into the crowd and completely froze in fear. I felt like I was going to have a heart attack! I don't know how long I stood there, like a deer in headlights, but then the crowd started cheering. "You got this, RaNae!" came from somewhere and then it got louder, until it became the crowd chanting my name. Because of them, I snapped out of my fear and paralyzing coma, finishing my speech strong!

Unbreakable

Sometimes opportunities come to you when you least expect them. That happened to me when I was at one of my most pivotal points and it has changed my life forever. It also brought on the attack that almost ended my life.

Esther, a lady that I knew from work came up to me, and said, "RaNae, I know that you are a wonderful person. You have great personality and do amazing things. What's your plan for the future? Because they are going to close the foundry down."

"I don't know," I replied, surprised by the question. "All the plans I had don't make sense. I know one thing for sure: if it doesn't make money, it doesn't make sense."

She said to me, "My brother in law is coming next week. He's a millionaire down in Florida and he has a business opportunity that he wants us to look at. Why don't you come with me Thursday at 7pm?"

"Sure. I have never had a meeting with a millionaire before. I can't wait!"

I went with Esther and I realized this opportunity was not like anything ever seen before. It was revolutionary. It was a complete game changer. I didn't need a huge amount of start-up capital. It was something for the average person to use to make the *Rich Dad* crossover to Big Business and investing. I loved that it was modeled like a franchise but was a turn-key business with billion-dollar systems in place. I could easily tell it could not be duplicated and was like nothing the world had ever seen before. So, I registered my business. I didn't know it then, but it would change my life forever.

They had great training audios. I also started watching Jim Rohn videos and listening to Dani Johnson teachings to get inspired. I'm a fork lift driver. I know none of this. But I said to myself, "You didn't know how to operate a fork lift, and you learned. You didn't know how to build a car engine, but you've been doing it for nine years. If you can do anything a man can do, you can do this too!" So, I kept on studying. I was a slow starter and I decided that I wasn't going to talk to anyone until I could get handle on this.

A short time later, a male friend and I were scheduled to go to my first business conference. I was so looking forward to it. It finally felt like life was moving forward, but Satan has an evil way of trying to keep good from coming into your life. Thankfully, God spared me.

The conference was from Thursday—Saturday. I booked time off from Wednesday afternoon on so that we could get there and be ready to go. I was staying with a group of women in one hotel room and he was staying with a bunch of guys, but it was nice to have a travel companion. On Wednesday morning, I asked my boss if I could work through my morning break so I could leave a bit earlier. I still shiver about what happened next.

At that point, I was working on the line making head jacket molds that used poisonous gas as part of the manufacturing process. We wore specialized helmets that provided oxygen and sealed out the gas. Four people worked at a time and there was one spare relief-man to cover those who needed to go on break to ensure production did not stop.

Johnny (not his real name) came up to me and told me I was to take my first break at 9am.

"No, Johnny," I said. "I am not taking my first break today because I am leaving early. I am going on vacation today."

At 9am, he snarled, "Take a break. Now.'" We got into an argument. He came up to my machine and hit the emergency stop button to shut my machine down. Johnny scowled at me and said, "I told you, you are on break!"

I walked away from the area to talk to my boss who was watching from a catwalk bridge overlooking all the operations. I didn't realize that Johnny was following me. I said, "Hey, Boss, remember when you said that that I didn't have to take my break so I could leave early today? Johnny said I couldn't."

Johnny bellowed from behind me, "I told you THAT YOU WERE ON BREAK!"

I turned around and told Johnny that he wasn't the boss. Enraged, Johnny lunged at me and pinned me to the railing of that two-story catwalk bridge. The boss had to pull Johnny off me because I was trapped. I couldn't fight him. It was so sudden that he caught me off guard.

RaNae Envy

I said to my boss, "Thank you, thank you." I turned to Johnny and said, "I hope that you don't like your job." I was so mad and scared at the same time. It wouldn't have taken much for him to have pushed me over the railing, leaving me paralyzed or worse, dead.

The most disgusting part of this story came after. The union wanted to cover it all up! They said, "RaNae, is there any way that we can prevent this from being reported to Labor Relations? Can we just handle this?" I was furious! I was so angry and felt unprotected. I responded bitterly, "Yeah, you take him out back and hold him down and give me a metal pipe to swing at him!" They shook their heads, "Oh, RaNae, we can't let you do that!" I said, "Well then, you better meet me down in Labor!" I couldn't believe they would even give the suggestion of letting this incident slide.

The company fired him that same day and walked him out. On Monday when I returned to work, I found out that he had spent 17 years in jail for the murder of his first wife. He had shot her on their front lawn for cheating. My female co-worker showed me his court documents on the computer, because she was concerned for my safety. After that, I was petrified he would sneak back into the building to get his revenge. He knew my schedule and he knew exactly where I worked. Johnny also knew that I couldn't see anything behind me while I was wearing my fresh air helmet. I knew that he could easily kill me when I couldn't see him.

Neither the company nor the union would move me out of that part of the plant until 30 days later when they gave Johnny his job back. They moved me to the other side of the plant on a different shift because Johnny had more seniority than me. No one took it seriously, including my father. When I told my father what had happened and about my fear, he said, "Well you better see if they have bulletproof vests in the supplies area of the plant!" I had cried to the Union, "How can you leave me here, like a sitting duck? You know he's a convicted murderer!" But my pleas fell on deaf ears! I know that if my boss hadn't been there that day, I could have been DEAD!

So, the point I want to make in this chapter is this: if you're going through hell, keep on going! Another level, another devil. Life has a way of making you uncomfortable so that you will listen more to the dreams in your heart. You must think, "This is not happening to me. This is happening FOR ME!"

I am thankful. All the things that have happened to me have caused me to become so strong inside. These things could have buried me, but instead I let them become seeds. They became the seeds that caused me to grow and change to become an unstoppable person.

"I will not be another flower, picked for my beauty and left to die. I will be wild, difficult to find, and impossible to forget."

—*Erin Van Vuren*

I know that all my goals and dreams are within my grasp. Every day I am getting closer to realizing them and I would love for you to join me. Click here berichyou.com to find out more about how we can work together to make your life the way you want.

In the next chapter, I am going to share with you how my life has changed from that scared young woman to the woman I am today, a warrior princess.

CHAPTER 3

"Give a Girl the Right Shoes and She Can Conquer the World."

—*Marilyn Monroe*

ALMOST EVERY PERSON HAS HAD a turning point in their life, when they knew that something had to change. For some people, it can be something dramatic, like a heart attack or declaring bankruptcy. For others, it is something small, but it is a catalyst that starts the change.

For me, it was both. The times where I have been physically attacked certainly have had a profound effect on me, but it wasn't the turning point. For me, the turning came on an ordinary day, while I was standing at the machine wearing the fresh air hood, creating parts. It felt unhuman. I felt like I was more machine than alive. I was trapped and unable to get away. Imagine a flower in the middle of a poison factory, with a little hood around its head and a tube giving it just enough oxygen to stay alive.

I knew that there was so much more inside of me, and that job wasn't bringing it out. So, I started listening to inspirational recordings while I was working on that machine. The recordings were great and told me, "You can make it. You can do anything." I began reprogramming my brain while I was doing a job that didn't require a high level of concentration. Since we were allowed headphones while we worked, I took the worst part of my job and turned it into a blessing.

That was also the point when I decided to look for other income opportunities and I registered my business. At first, because I didn't have much confidence in myself, I didn't do much. Still, I spent a lot of time learning. All those hours of listening to people, like Jim Rohn, at work was instilling in me the courage to take risks and be bold.

The day came when I knew it was "do or die." I had to start moving forward in my business and promoting it. I started doing events, even though I wasn't fully prepared for them. One of the divisions in my business is cosmetics, so I started with that because it was easy. I didn't have all the makeup, but I went and did my first event using only my own personal makeup from my makeup bag to showcase our products and catalogs.

Most people would have said, "I can't do that because I don't have all the makeup. I'm not fully prepared," or "They're gonna know I don't know anything." I was willing to take the risk and do something new.

When you step out of your fear and try something new, you will realize that you had nothing to be afraid of. That's when the magic happens. It was a good day. People bought my products and I felt like I was accomplished! I thought, "If I could make progress with just what little I had, imagine how much more progress I could make if I had everything!" The potential to grow excited me and gave me energy.

Henry Ford said it best. "Whether you believe you can, or you believe that you can't, you are right." For me, there was a progression from fear to confidence. First, I made the decision that things had to change. Then I started to reprogram my brain for success. As my confidence grew, it gave me the courage to start taking small risks. Those small risks confirmed my belief in myself and I moved forward in life to take bigger risks.

Then the entire process starts all over again, moving me higher and higher. Think of a whirlwind, and its continuing upward motion. As I began to move upward, something amazing happened: more opportunities began to open up for me.

I started mentoring a young man who had made some contacts in the fashion industry. He said to me, "RaNae, I have a friend who is a designer in New York City, and he's doing a fashion show for Fashion Week. Can we do it? Can we go?"

"Well, see if they need any more makeup artists." That was the first Fashion Week fashion show that I had ever done. After that, I was travelling back and forth to New York on a regular basis. I was doing fashions shows and photo shoots. I even did a video for a recording artist.

At this point, I had the entire cosmetic line, including custom blend foundation and powder systems that allowed me to create custom cosmetic solutions, which were unlike anything offered by any other cosmetic company.

I decided to put on my own Makeup Artist Workshop in Brooklyn, New York. I rented a studio, partnered up with a photographer, and had 8 volunteer models. I rented an apartment and took 4 young makeup and hair stylists from Ohio with me. It was amazing to instill the belief into these 4 young kids from Ohio that they could do anything they put their minds to. They called me their 'Makeup Mommy!' In my mind, that was more important than any of the money I had made. I was truly making a difference in other people's lives.

Some months later I ran into a guy that I had known, and he said, "RaNae! Oh my gosh, my ex-girlfriend told me that you're a makeup artist in New York City! I told her, 'No way. RaNae? Dirty RaNae that works in the foundry?'"

He shook his head. "I said to her, 'You're telling me that RaNae is a makeup artist in New York City?' 'Yeah,' she said and she showed me your Facebook."

"How did you go from working in a dirty factory to a makeup artist in New York City?" he asked.

"I don't know." I replied. "It's the craziest thing. I just went for it and magic happened. I'm just following God/Creator's plan. His path."

The Pursuit of Happiness

Now I must admit to you, there was one small advantage to working in a car manufacturing plant for a long time. I was making a very good wage. While it was way more than average, I can tell you this: the mental, emotional, and physical toll makes you wonder if it was worth the pay. However, the mental toughness you develop will help you to achieve greatness.

I had many girlfriends that wished they made the money I did. When they would ask me if I could get them a job, I told them that I couldn't. When I was hired was the last time there were positions open, and we had a slow and steady decline in jobs since then. It was like our whole careers were spent just holding on to what jobs we did have. When I first started in 1999, we had 4 operating and prosperous plants, that included two engine plants, one aluminum plant and one cast iron foundry. The carnage of the decline of the American economy closed 3 out of 4 of our plants. By 2012, the Iron Casting Plant was completely torn down and gone! Not only that, but I wouldn't want any of my girlfriends to have to go through a lot of what I went through.

So, having money did help when I started my business, but not everyone starts where I started. Here's the thing: it doesn't matter where you start, you just HAVE to start, and you can reach success.

Start treating your mind with positivity. One of the most amazing books on the planet is *The Greatest Salesman in the*

World by Og Mandino. (Honestly, the title doesn't match the true power of the book.) That book is still changing my life. Also, Robert Kiyosaki's books, *Rich Dad, Poor Dad* and *The Cash Flow Quadrant,* gave me the knowledge to grow financially. My dad gave me those two books when I was 17. It was a positive seed that my dad planted early in my life that is still bearing fruit today.

"Those who seek . . . Find!" Success leaves clues for you to find it. If you go searching for them, they will come at the right time. You will find the books and teachings that meet you right where you are and will give you the tools to move forward. You will hear inspiring stories of people who have been where you are and made their dreams a reality or overcame the same obstacle you are facing.

For me, I also found inspiration in Steve Harvey's story. Years ago, the comedian had worked at the exact same company and plant that I did.

In 2015, the city of Cleveland named a portion of E.112th Street as "Steve Harvey Way" in honor of his 58th birthday. The car company put out a leaflet saying that they were looking for people who had worked with Steve Harvey. I kept that leaflet and made copies of it. I put it in places where I would see it every day and told myself, "If he can make it, I can make it!"

Two years later, Steve had a YouTube video talking about "your paper" and a very important lesson.

When he was a young boy, he had gotten in trouble in school for being a smart aleck. When his father had come home his mother told him, "Your son has been acting up in school today." Then his mother told Steve to tell his dad what he wrote for his school paper, whose topic was "What do you want to be when you grow up?"

He answered, "I want to be on T.V.!"

His father asked his mother, "Well, what's wrong with that?"

His mother responded, "Well, he's been a smart aleck, writing something so unbelievable on his paper!" They continued to argue, and Steve was sent to his bedroom.

After everything had settled down, his dad went into his room and said, "Alright, this is what we are going to do. What does the teacher want you to put?"

Steve answered, "I don't know Daddy, maybe like a basketball player or something like what the rest of the kids wrote!"

His father said, "Ok well, put that on your paper and take that to school with you tomorrow. But take this paper and put it in your drawer. Every morning when you wake up, read your paper. And every night before you go to bed, read your paper. THAT IS YOUR PAPER!"

What his dad told him was a principle of success. That if you write it down, and envision it, then anything you can see in your mind, you can hold in your hand!

After Steve made it on T.V., every year for Christmas during her lifetime, he would send that teacher a brand new T.V. because he wanted her to see that he was on T.V. Against all odds, the little boy with a stuttering problem made it on T.V.

The information you need is at hand. Once you have made it a part of you, it's going to take some sweat equity. It's going to take sacrifice. That's probably what stops most people, because they are afraid of change and afraid they won't make it, so they don't even try.

A funny thing happened when I started seeing success in my business. I could handle working at the car plant better. My circumstances at the car plant didn't change, but suddenly, I didn't feel so trapped. I had hope and that allowed me to see things differently. That job was no longer a controlling factor in my life.

> *"When you change the way you look at things,*
> *the things you look at change."*
> —*Wayne Dyer*

There were other effects after I started my own business. I got to travel to business conferences, and I have more friends from all over the world. It opened up the world to me. I am the creator of my destiny, rather than feeling bad about not fully loving my life.

I am finally free to be the woman I am meant to be. Now, when I go to conferences or meetings, I wear pretty dresses and heels. People ask me, "What do you do for a living?"

My answer is always the same, "Well, you're not going to believe it, but I'm a forklift driver. . . . and I build engines." They are astonished. I say, "It's true, but I also have my own business because it gives me the opportunity to be feminine and wear dresses."

My success comes from the fact I am not limited in the type of products that I offer, because my company is a product brokerage. Going into business for yourself with a plan rooted in product brokerage is an excellent way to provide the best products to your customers and always remain ahead of the trends.

One of the most advantageous aspects of my company's Shop. com's business model is that the company doesn't manufacture any products or specialize in a single service, which allows us to swing with the marketplace and capitalize on current consumer demands.

Unlike many niche companies that live or die by the success of one product, Shop.com is able to offer a variety of products and brands across numerous multibillion-dollar markets. From health and nutrition to cosmetics, weight management to home and garden, they will always provide the most popular products.

This flexibility ensures stability, profitability, and most importantly, longevity.

The product brokerage concept carries far beyond exclusive brands. Through Shop.com/rich, the company can offer millions of additional products and services from well-known stores, like Target, Nike, Apple, Home Depot and more.

The cost is the same as it would be shopping directly from the store's site, but Shop.com/rich pays cashback, whereas individual sites do not.

When I first started my business, I began with the cosmetic sales because it was something I knew, so it was easy. It was also very rewarding to make another woman feel beautiful.

I wasn't limited to what type of products I had to offer, so I could help virtually anyone. It wasn't long until a doctor friend contacted me and asked, "Is this Shop.com something I can do? I really need to increase my income!" I told her, "Yes, we actually have an exclusive line of nutraceuticals just for doctors, but I have to become certified through the company as a nutraceutical rep." Within a few months, we both were scheduled for the specialized training. I found myself being trained alongside doctors.

Let me remind you, I had only had two quarters of college, but found that with this opportunity, the doors opening for me were limitless.

I would come back to work and talk with my co-workers about everything I was experiencing. Some of them wanted to try different products. Some men would buy nutraceuticals, and some women would buy makeup from me. Some days, I was getting paid to go to work and deliver the products.

Interestingly enough, working from home is becoming the next major movement in our country to reach financial success.

The products my company sells (you can check them out for yourself at www.shop.com/rich) have made a difference in my life. The (Isotonix) nutraceuticals have improved my health. One of my favorite products keeps my immune system strong, so when an infection tries to take over, I can take it. Within a very short space of time, I start to feel better.

It is in isotonic form, which means that when you take it, the nutraceuticals go straight into your bloodstream within 5-10 minutes. Your body recognizes it as something that it has created, and the bio-availability is through the roof. If you would like to find out more about these amazing products, then click here. www.shop.com/rich.

One of the biggest personal changes I have experienced from owning my own business is that I am no longer self-serving.

When I found the business opportunity that transformed over 400 average people—men and women from all walks of life—into millionaires, I realized that my job was self-serving. It's actually selfish to choose to stay at the level where you are at, because there are so many other people who need to change their lives. I saw that I could be an agent of change for others like myself. You have to succeed so that others can believe they too can succeed.

Starting Point

If you want to change your life, then you have to do something different. You must find ways create additional income that does not rely on other people. When you have a job, other people control your financial future. That means your income can be yanked away from you at any time. I have seen too many people walk into work one day, thinking everything is secure, and by the end of the day, their job no longer exists.

These jobs are not loyal, and you shouldn't be either. You must have other sources of income to secure your future. Dig your well, before you are thirsty.

There are many ways of adding income. We are not going to explore them here because that is a book in and of itself. I suggest that you start researching and investigating them right now as part of your path to create change.

I researched the businesses that would offer the biggest return on my investment and provide the most opportunities to change my life and the lives of others as well. Like in *Cashflow Quadrant*, I knew I wanted to be focused on the Big Business and Investor side of the quadrant. I highly recommend that you check it out by clicking here www.shoppingannuity.com/rich.

Besides acquiring additional sources of income, there will be other changes you have to make. In some cases, you will have to change your circle. The higher the goal you set, the sooner you are going to realize there are people in your life that do not want you to have more than what you already have. They cannot imagine living any differently than they do now, so they don't see the possibilities. Like Jim Rohn said, "You are the average of the five people you spend the most time with."

Imagine being on a football team. You made a commitment to the team, so you sacrifice free time with your friends for football practice. Your friends may say, "Why don't you hang out with us anymore? Come and play video games with us." You have become successful with football and you see the powerful and positive effects it has on your life. You don't want to give that up for video games. When you change, your circle must change too.

The more that you search for wisdom, the more you will understand that it is truly an unlimited life. Then you begin to realize who's really 100% on your team. It might be hurtful to learn that your family or your closest loved ones aren't always on your team. It is not because they don't love you. It is because they are not into playing football.

They don't have the vision. They don't have that voice inside of them that is God/Creator talking to you. You can't share your vision with everybody because they won't all understand. You must appreciate that most people can only comprehend from their level of understanding at that time. You may have heard the phrase, "I am responsible for what I say, not for what you understand." Millionaires can't yet understand Billionaire problems, let alone solve them. Billionaires can't fathom Trillionaire problems, let alone solve them.

You must grow into the person who can solve these types of problems to earn these types of incomes. You don't have to follow their same path, but you have to stretch your thinking beyond where you have ever stretched it before. A mind once stretched can never go back to its old dimensions.

A great tool for keeping your vision in front of you is to write it down. At this point, you don't have to know how you will make it happen. You just have to know where you want to be in the future. Write down exactly what you want your life to look like in detail. Write it as if you were writing a fairy tale, a novel, or a letter to Santa Claus but Santa Claus is God/Creator.

Take some time to think about how it would feel, and what it would look like, and write it down. Heck, dream in real daylight and test drive that dream car or walk through that open house of your dream home. Touch your dreams so you know they are real, touchable, acquirable things.

Take pictures, print them out, and create a dream board/ movie poster of your upcoming life/movie. Write out the movie preview and put it next to your dream board/ movie poster. Read it every day, first thing in the morning and before you go to sleep at night. You can't imagine how it is going to all pan out.

It's the power of writing your own story. Your life right now might be on Chapter 5. Write down what you would want Chapter 8 to look like. Every great movie has an underdog challenge or a villain preventing the happy ever after! If you are not to your happy ever after yet, you are just at the part that makes the movie worth watching. No guts, no glory!

There is a transformative video by Jim Rohn called, The Day That Turns Your Life Around. It is worth watching. Do you want to hear something crazy? I have listened to that audio countless times. However, it wasn't until I went to Raymond Aaron's Brand Your Way to Wealth seminar that the message clicked in my brain and my life changed. Sometimes, you must hear the same message from different people before you fully understand the magnitude of the words. It is like in that moment the words become alive and you can internalize them.

Superman

Now is the time to make the choice to be the superman or superwoman of your own life. You can choose your path and you can achieve the success that you desire. Make today the turning point where your life changes and starts to become the life you want it to be. I would love to personally help you with that.

Go to berichyou.com to find out how I can help you to live the life of your dreams.

I wish I could tell you that your road to success would be straight without hills or obstacles, but that would be a lie. No one has ever accomplished anything great without facing adversity. No one successful will tell you that it was always easy. They struggled at times, had to learn new skills, and sometimes failed, but they never gave up. That is why they are where they are today.

When you do the impossible, then you show others it is possible.

A great example of that idea came from one of the old timers that would visit me while I worked. Many years ago, he gotten a job bid for the knock-out house.

The knock-out house was a close-knit set of guys that didn't let anyone just come into the department. They had one of the hardest jobs, so the ergonomic protection for the job was one hour on and one hour off.

These men had to swing a large sledgehammer and hit a certain spot on the massive iron block that was poured hours ago. The main component of an engine is the engine block. It would be your torso and rib cage on a human. The blocks would be poured and then hooked up to a chain in the ceiling to take the block to the other side of the building for shipping but also it was a 3-hour chain from hook up to knock off to let the iron cool down enough for a human to come close to it.

These men had to hit the block in a very precise way and close to the chain. Then it would drop into a pan, and then into a shaker.

Randy was the new guy and they were not going to show him the trick to the trade. Instead, they decided to let the new guy swing himself right out of the department.

After hours of frustration, he told me he looked at all those guys and said, "Ain't none of you, Superman! NONE OF YOU ARE SUPERMAN! I'm going to figure out what the trick is, so ya better get used to me!"

He figured it out. Sometimes you will be tested just to see how bad you really want it. Breaking limiting beliefs feels amazing.

"I used to be embarrassed because I was just a comic-book writer while other people were building bridges or going on to medical careers. And then I began to realize: entertainment is one of the most important things in people's lives. Without it they might go off the deep end. I feel that if you're able to entertain people, you're doing a good thing."

—*Stan Lee creator of Marvel comics*

In the next chapter I am going to show you the common pitfalls that every successful person encounters and how you can either avoid them or quickly get through them so they won't hinder your success.

Knowledge is power. When you know what you are facing, it makes it a lot easier to handle. As you learn from others who have been there before you, then you realize that nothing is impossible for those who believe. You don't know what you don't know. Once you know, everything changes!

CHAPTER 4

"The Airplane Takes Off Against The Wind, Not With It."

—*Henry Ford*

THE ROAD TO SUCCESS IN life is paved with . . . OBSTACLES. You were probably hoping that I was going to say something like an endless path of soft grass or warm sand that gently massages your feet as you walk. Believe me, I wish I could tell you that.

Everything worthwhile that you do in this life has a cost to it. As Jim Rohn says, "Success is something you attract by the person you become." As hard as it may be to hear, if you aren't ready for success, it won't come near you.

> *"To each there comes in their lifetime a special moment when they are figuratively tapped on the shoulder and offered the chance to do a very special thing, unique to them and fitted to their talents. What a tragedy if that moment finds them unprepared or unqualified for that which could have been their finest hour."*
> —*Sir Winston Churchill*

There is also an enemy to your success, who doesn't want anyone to succeed in life. His goal is to do everything he can to distract, discourage, bully, and tire you out so that you never reach your goals and your dreams. So, if all these things are against you, how are you ever going to achieve success?

One of the keys to overcoming any hurdle is knowledge. Knowing is half the battle. When you are aware of what is going on, the process of conquering any obstacle, trial, or problem becomes easier and faster.

Soul Surfer

I can truly say it feels like all hell has broken loose since I started to write this book. The enemy doesn't want this message reaching your ears because it will change your life.

It started earlier this year when I decided that I needed to share my experience to encourage others to persevere. The opportunity came for me to write this book. Then I was unlawfully pulled over by a police officer, detained, and falsely charged with an automatic license suspension for a refusal to blow, when I had 2 unregistered blow receipts. It is them vs. you.

It felt like frustration was my constant companion. It has been a lengthy battle to prove my innocence and it did delay slightly the writing of this book. However, I can tell you that good prevailed and the charges were dropped with prejudice.

Isn't that discouraging?

But . . .

No sooner did I get my license back, then my car was hijacked while my good friend drove it to run and grab a pizza. Everything in my car was stolen, including my computer with all the notes for this book.

Keep in mind, this car was my new accolade. My first brand new Mercedes. I had only had it 45 days when the police stole it. Then I had just had it 2 weeks and my friend had a gun put to his head, along with demands to "Give me the car!" Jealousy is a sin and it turns people ugly. We should inspire and help each other but that has not been happening.

Reminds me of the Janis Joplin song , . . .

"Oh Lord, won't you buy me a Mercedes Benz? My friends all drive Porsches, I must make amends, Worked hard all my lifetime, no help from my friends, So oh Lord, won't you buy me a Mercedes Benz?"

One lesson I learned was to always double back-up anything that is important to me on a regular basis! I am grateful I got my car back within a week. The Cleveland Police had found it within 19 hours, but then it had to go for fingerprinting and to be processed for evidence. Losing my computer was hard, but I am more thankful that my friend wasn't hurt. Things can be replaced, people can't. I love my friend dearly and I am so grateful he is safe.

While these things were happening, I had a choice to make. I could let these things drag me down and never write another word, or I could choose to look at them as temporary storms that will pass to allow me to move forward. Obviously, you can guess which one I chose!

Before we get into overcoming obstacles, there is one thing I want to cover. Not everything that happens is meant to stop you. Many times, I believe that God/Creator gives you a problem so you can step-up and be the champion of it. Sometimes, God/Creator is pushing you in the direction that you need to go in because you wouldn't move or budge without a huge nudge from the universe. Those problems are not meant to frustrate you but help you to grow.

It is important to recognize where the problem is coming from. If you ignore a problem that is meant for your growth, then you will lose. If you become obsessed with a problem that is meant to take you down, the you will lose. The key is to find the balance that allows you to learn and grow from the problems that present themselves.

Let me give you two examples. Alice is a make-up artist. She ran into a situation where God/Creator wanted her to grow her level of influence by offering a new service. She didn't feel ready because it would require the purchase of new equipment, so she sent the customers to another makeup artist, Betty.

One customer came back and told Alice about the horrible service she had received from Betty. As she talked, Alice realized that she could have done a better job. She also realized that this was the push she needed to grow into the next level God had waiting for her.

The other example is what I like to call "the crab mentality." When you have crabs in a bucket, and one tries to escape, the others will pull it back into the bucket and not allow it to leave. The philosophy is that if they (the group of crabs) can't have something, then they are not going to let anyone else have it either. As you move forward, there will be people who will be jealous of your ambition and determination. They will try to drag you back. Many times, these are the people who are closest to you and the ones who should be cheering you on instead of holding you back.

In that case, it is an obstacle that you need to release. Sometimes, you need to leave those who do not support you behind. Don't let others determine your destiny.

Against All Odds

When it comes to reaching your goals and dreams, there are two types of resistance, internal and external. It is hard to say which one is more difficult or challenging, but I tend to believe that what goes on internally can be a greater hindrance than anything on the outside. When your inner man is strong, you are generally able to overcome the problems and obstacles offered by the outside world.

"When there is no enemy within,
the enemy outside can do us no harm."

—*African Proverb*

Inner Issues

The biggest issue most people face is fear. Fear of failure, fear of success, fear of people, and so on. The list is endless. This world's system is designed to raise you up in fear so that those in power make money. If you watch carefully, you will see that most media messages are designed to make you afraid of what might happen if you don't do what they want.

How do you know if there is fear in your life? Sometimes it can be so ingrained that you don't even recognize its presence. Take a look at this list and see if you recognize yourself in it. The more things you see in yourself, the greater your level of fear.

- You worry about what people think of you.
- You don't like trying new things.
- You don't believe you can accomplish things.
- You always tell people what you can't do, so their expectations will be lower, and you won't fail.
- You suddenly feel 'sick' and back out of things that you think are too hard.

- You procrastinate often.

- You have a challenging time making decisions because it might be the wrong one.

- You sabotage yourself, so you have an excuse for why you can't complete something.

- You can't handle any type of constructive criticism because you think that it is a personal attack.

How do you conquer fear? The first step is to learn to recognize fear. Most people think that their fears are real, but what they come to realize is that fear is a programmed response from childhood. You were taught to be afraid. Over time, it grew to the point that it now paralyzes you, thus keeping you from reaching your full potential.

Second, take small steps to bravery. When my friend Kim started to battle her fear, she had to do it one step at a time. She had been told as a child that she wasn't a good writer and she believed it. Over time, she came to believe that the best she could be at any task was average. So average in fact, she thought of herself as invisible.

When she was 40-years-old, Kim had an opportunity to write professionally. Everything inside of her screamed, "No! Don't do it!! You can't write. No one will like it. Everyone will know how horrible you are. At least when you are invisible, no one pays attention to you and you are safe. Stay that way. That way is better." On and on it went.

But . . .

The still, small voice of God/Creator was there too, encouraging her to try. So, with the little bit of courage that she had, she wrote a half page blog post by hand. Only a few hundred words, but she submitted it and waited for the laughter to begin.

Kim was so surprised when she was told that her writing was good, and people wanted to see more. This response led to more blog posts and then guest posts on other sites. Then the next big level came when she realized that she had a book in her.

At that point, fear tried to take over again. It wasn't as strong as the first time, but it still took a while before Kim could overcome it. When she did, the results were amazing. Now when Kim goes to events, people who have read her book recognize her and they come up to talk to her.

The ultimate step to overcoming her fear of writing happened almost two years ago, when Kim had an opportunity to write for other people. This time the battle lasted less than a day. Now Kim makes a full-time living helping others to become authors themselves. All because she took that first step and then all those little steps of bravery, which leads to . . .

The third step is to remember that you don't need a lot of courage to take that first step. Here is the thing about courage: a little goes a long way. Just make the decision to take that first, tiny step and watch how your courage grows. You find you have the courage to take another tiny step, perhaps just a little bit bigger. Then you take another step and another. Soon, you are taking bigger and bigger steps until you are running. Finally, you fly.

External Issues

As you move towards success, every circumstance and obstacle, which can come against you, will. You are on your way to an important meeting and your tire goes flat. Your kid throws up on your new suit just as you are going out the door. Your computer is hacked and held ransom. All the money for advertising your business now goes to a criminal, just to keep your business running. Crazy things will happen.

How do you deal with it all, especially when it seems like one thing after another? You take a deep breath, and ask yourself, "What is my next best move?" Remember that "this too shall pass," and continue on. Do what you can and then let go of the rest. What is your next best move? The one that gives you your power back. You need to think, "What IS in my power that will make this situation better?" Once you can get that done, then look for the next move that is in your power. Now you have accomplished something, and the situation loses its power over you.

Sometimes I ask people to name one problem or terrible situation that they have NOT made it through yet. Nobody can answer that question, because they have survived everything to this point, or they wouldn't be here to answer that question! What that question shows us is that all our problems are only temporary illusions.

Miracle

"There are two ways to live: you can live as if nothing is a miracle; you can live as if everything is a miracle."

—*Albert Einstein*

As we end this chapter, I want you to know that you are a miracle. There is literally one chance out of 400 trillion of becoming a human rather than a tree.

Dr. Seuss said, "I've heard there are troubles of more than one kind; some come from ahead, and some come from behind. But I've brought a big bat. I'm all ready, you see; now my troubles are going to have troubles with me!"

Don't let anything stop from reaching your goals and dreams. I can't believe how full my life has become now by letting go of the things that held me back. Every day I reach more and more of my goals. This book is one of my dreams come true and I hope that it has been of help to you. I would love to have the opportunity to work with you personally. Go to www.envyfactor.com/apprentice.

CHAPTER 5

"Ours Is Not To Reason Why,
Ours Is But To Do or Die."

—*Alfred Lord Tennyson*

I AM VERY PROUD TO SHARE that within the last few years our Shop.com -Motives Makeup team has donated our makeup services to the Miss Wheelchair USA Pageant! These women are beyond inspirational and beautiful! I absolutely must share with you the newly crowned Miss Wheelchair USA 2017 - Miss Madeline Delp's powerful story in her own words:

There are details about my story that I rarely ever tell people, but I am going to share them with you. One night when I was ten years old, my mother and I decided to watch a movie together on the Disney channel about a boy who used a wheelchair. It was the first time I had ever really thought about what it would be like to not be able to walk. I remember lying awake late that night thinking about how terrible and unfathomably difficult that would be to go through . . .

Exactly one week later, my mother and I were in a car accident. When I regained consciousness in a hospital bed, they told me that I had been paralyzed from the waist down and would never walk again.

It just goes to show that sometimes things happen in our lives that we never in a million years would think would happen to us.

Until they do—and we are left to pick up the pieces and figure out how we are going to move on.

Let's take a step back. For most of my life, it had just been my mom and I. After my parents divorced, my father remarried and while I saw him and his new family every other weekend, for the most part it was Mom and I taking on the world together. We had already faced some challenges trying to get to the stable place that we were in. It seemed we had finally come to the light at the end of the tunnel. I was at a great school, we had a church support group that surrounded us, and we had just bought a new house. Things were looking up. But destiny seemed to have a different plan.

We were driving home from church after rehearsing a song to sing the following Sunday, when we were hit by a truck. The back of the car collapsed on top of me and I was thrown forward so violently that the seatbelt smashed against my spine. I was very badly injured and bleeding so profusely that the doctors didn't expect me to live through the night—but somehow, I survived.

After months of being in a rehabilitation hospital, I could finally return home. Home, to a house that I couldn't get into, because there were too many stairs. Home, to a school that said they would make no adaptations to be accessible for me to continue to attend. Home, to a church that said the car accident had been punishment for a sin of my own. Home: where the people who were closest to us suddenly turned their backs on us. I felt like my entire world had rejected me. In my darkest hour, I would look up to the sky and ask God, "Why didn't you just let me die?"

While the numerous physical challenges I was facing were certainly difficult, it was the emotional pain that was breaking me down. I would smile to the world all day long but would never let anyone see the demons I was fighting inside. It was as though I had become ashamed of what had happened—ashamed of who I was. I felt like I was such a burden on others that I was constantly afraid of how they would react to me. Fear began to control my life, I withdrew from trying new things, from pursuing new interactions—even from speaking too loud. I was afraid of making others uncomfortable at the mere mention of my situation. My disability wasn't that I used a wheelchair, my disability came from my paralyzing fear.

After years of being held back by fear, the day came when I knew that there had to be something more. When I was fifteen, I went to a Spinal Cord Injury recovery center in Detroit. At the time, my stepfather had become abusive to my mother and we needed a place of escape. A planned three-month stay turned into a year, and while it was intended to help my muscles get stronger, it became just as much a period of emotional healing.

I met people who I could relate to and share my story with, and I didn't feel so alone. After returning home, I began the journey of finding my voice and building confidence in myself. I was finally seeing the amazing potential of a life I could live beyond the fear and shame—a life where I wasn't bound to the scars of my past.

Through my self-awareness, my eyes were, in turn, opened to the pain that so many others in similar situations were experiencing. I wanted to find a way where I could inspire people struggling and hurting from "disabling" life circumstances to shed their bounds and live a life beyond the pain of past experiences. I wanted to show how I had found healing and had fought to live a full, healthy and vibrant life. Hopefully, my story might motivate them to believe that they too, could do the same. Through this passion, Live Boundless was born.

I have spent the past several years filming inspirational materials to promote the "boundless" mindset. Now, as Ms. Wheelchair USA, I have the chance to take my advocacy to the next level. I am partnering with a production team in Wilmington, NC to film a 25-Part Live Boundless series that will educate wheelchair users on how to adapt to each area of life, meanwhile inspiring people from all backgrounds that no matter what their "disability" may be, they too have the strength to overcome.

The series will cover all areas of life—from learning adaptive driving to showing the process of recovery to working towards walking again, to doing adaptive surfing or skydiving. The main theme being that you are not bound to your circumstances—it is your response to those circumstances that will be the deciding factor in whether you let them limit you or not.

We are about to embark on an incredible journey of traveling around the nation to show how to create an unstoppable mentality and make the most of whatever we are given in this life. Tell me, are you ready to LIVE BOUNDLESS?

We Are Marshall

I have something to confess to you. I didn't always understand the role of commitment in becoming successful. Like most people, commitment felt like a bad word that you avoided because it conjured up visions of never-ending work and boredom. Then I learned the truth and commitment changed my life. I know that it can change your life, too!

The movie *We Are Marshall* is an excellent example of how commitment can not only make a difference in one person's life, but to an entire community. In 1970, almost the entire football team, coaches, and supporters of a college were killed in a horrific plane crash in the U.S. The town was devastated and suffering greatly.

In 1971, a new coach, Jack Lengyel, comes on the scene. He is a newcomer with a vision to rebuild the team and heal the town. So many obstacles were in his way, but he made the commitment to make it work. In the end, he helped the remaining team members and the surviving assistant coach come to terms with their survivors' guilt and helped the town find hope again.

He could have given up or given in to the pressure from those who couldn't let go of the past, but he saw what could be in the future and chose to focus on that.

Places Of The Heart

What is commitment? It is the decision to do something no matter what the cost. It is a "do or die" attitude that just won't quit. I like to compare it to breathing. Some commitments you can make subconsciously without thinking about actually "doing" them that allow you to truly live. Without it, you die. You won't physically die if you don't have commitment in your life, but your hopes, your dreams, and your ability to live the life that you want will.

Here is an important concept when it comes to commitment: If you don't sacrifice for what you want, what you WANTED BECOMES THE SACRIFICE!! The average person doesn't think that they have it in themselves to succeed, that it will take too long, or it will never happen. So, they settle for a JOB (or whatever employment that uses a skill set that they have as a passing talent) instead of pursuing their dream.

Time is going to pass, anyway. Unless you are injured or ill, you are going to work for over twenty years, whether that be at a job or staying at home with the kids. You will be doing something with your time, so why not make it profitable? The reason most people don't act this way is they have lost their commitment to themselves. We are sold on a commitment to a company. We are sold on a commitment to work at our jobs. We become loyal to the company, but ask yourself: is the company loyal to you?

Do you have something inside of you that is waiting to be accomplished? At the end of your days, will you look back on a full life or will you live in regret? You need to decide now that you will be committed to living YOUR life. Take a day and ask yourself, "What am I committing to myself? If I want everything a certain way, what would I need to commit to in order to get it that way?" Maybe your vision for success includes owning a business, becoming an artist, or making a difference in peoples' lives in some tangible way. Whatever your dream is, now is the time to start working towards it!

"Do or do not. There is no try."

—*Yoda*

When I hear someone say, "I'll try," I know that really means that they are absolutely, positively not going to do it, AND they are telling themselves and others that they are NOT going to do it! For example, you invite me to a party, and I say to you, "I will try to make it." Do you expect me to show up? Most likely not. You know that is my polite way of saying 'no' without hurting your feelings.

'Trying' is your excuse for not doing something. 'Try' makes you feel completely comfortable with your inaction. It's socially acceptable since you didn't (fully) lie to yourself or to anyone else! 'Try' has become a completely acceptable pretense in society. 'Try' is a participation reward. Try is almost! Have you ever 'almost' won the lottery and became a millionaire? On Monday, did you 'try' to pay any of your bills with that 'almost' lottery money? I doubt it!

'Try' sounds good in theory, but it is worthless in practice. You may be miserable in your job and hate it, so you decide to 'look' for something else. You work on your resume, but you don't put much time into it. Then you go online and apply for five jobs with the same resume for each. That's it—no research on the businesses or tailoring a cover letter to communicate your interest to future employers. When you don't hear back from any of the companies, then you think to yourself, "Well I *tried* to find work, but nobody wanted me."

You attempted to get a new job or career, but you missed key elements to make you get noticed by potential employers, like customizing your resume and taking courses on a regular basis to show that you are teachable. Someone, who is committed to getting the *right* job for them, will research their employers and continually seek to improve their skill set. The little extras will make them rise to the top of the list.

Feelings

Before we get into the basics of how to stay devoted to your goals and achieve success, there is one more thing we need to cover.

Commitment is not a feeling!!!

Commitment has nothing to do with emotions. It has everything to do with choice. When you think of commitment as a feeling, you doom yourself to failure before you even start.

Your feelings can change from minute to minute. Life can be great one moment and then the next smallest obstacle can leave you feeling like a failure without hope. There are going to be days when you don't feel committed, but you are still going to show up.

Let me share a story with you from Georgia B. All her life, Georgia felt average and invisible. While she had big dreams of being "somebody, some day," she never did anything to move towards it. Fear and condemnation were her closest friends. Any time she tried to move forward, one of those two 'friends' would work to convince her that she didn't have what it took to be successful at anything. Then she would stop trying.

This process went on well into her adulthood, but her hunger to be and do more was growing. She started to get the mindset teaching necessary to take those first few steps forward. It took a while for Georgia to finally understand, but the day came when she knew she had to make a choice. It was time to kick those so-called "friends" of hers to the curb and start a new friendship with commitment or keep those "friends" and never go anywhere.

It was hard. Fear and condemnation pulled every dirty trick they could to keep their hold on her. Fear told Georgia that if she took even one more step, she would fail and it would confirm what people already thought of her, "That she was a failure." Condemnation whispered into her soul that she was taking too much risk and her family would pay the price for her foolishness.

But . . .

Commitment was speaking to her as a still, small voice that told her that she could do it. It told Georgia that she wasn't a failure and the risk would pay off. Thankfully, fear and condemnation were sent packing and her relationship with commitment became permanent.

Want to know what happened? She now lives her dream of being a well-paid author and ghostwriter. Georgia publishes her own books and works collaboratively with other professionals to help them get their vitally needed messages out into the world. Why? Because she no longer listened to those emotions that told her she couldn't. Instead, she made the choice to be committed to a course of action until she saw success.

Unbroken

When you follow these basics of a committed life, then you are going to find your life full of continuous and unbroken growth. Things will get better and better. Obstacles, which once completely stopped you, no longer even cause you to pause.

How to stay committed when things get tough? First, don't make decisions when you are emotionally upset. That is when you are most tempted to quit. Find a place where you can get quiet and think things through. Is it really as bad as it seems, or are you reacting this way because of external forces, like fatigue? Everything looks worse when you are tired.

Second, remember why you are doing this. What is your goal? What will your life look like when you reach that goal, compared to now? This is the value of writing out your goals. Is your goal worth what you are going through?

Third, you must think of solutions, not focus on the problem. When you focus in on the problem, it becomes bigger. When you focus on the solution, the problem will go away. Ask yourself, "What is the best solution to this problem?" and then start writing down ideas. If you are stuck, then go to others and ask them for help. You will be amazed at what they come up with.

Remember Georgia? One of the things she did was talk to other people. When she came up against a problem she could not solve, then she would Google it. She would talk to her husband Rick about it. She would find inexpensive courses in her price range and buy them. Between those three things, many times the solution would present itself.

Fourth, make the choice to continue. You may find this hard, especially if you are used to giving up. Instead, choose to do one small thing that will move you towards your goal. Every time you do this, it will strengthen your resolve. As you see the results of meeting these "mini-goals", growth happens, and you will be motivated to accomplish more and more. Then you will see the progress you made by choosing to continue.

Fifth, keep a gratitude journal. This one is powerful. Every time you have a problem, write it down. Then spend time thanking and giving gratitude to God or your Source for solving this issue for your highest and best good. Thank Him for guiding your footsteps! Every time you overcome, thank Him. Every time you succeed, thank Him. Every time a problem presents itself and you figure it out, write it down and give thanks. If you feel discouraged or just need to reflect, then go back to your gratitude journal and read it. I just did this the other day. I was amazed at how many of the things I had written down ended up becoming reality! It wasn't always in MY timing, but in divine timing! It is also beneficial to remember all the times you thought something was impossible and you did it anyway. Encourage yourself to take the next step. Use past success to motivate you to take on new challenges.

The Finishers

I have made a commitment to myself to become financially free and every day I am working towards that goal. Do I have rough days? Sure, I do. Have I faced obstacles? You know I have, because I've shared them with you. Is there anything that is going to stop me from reaching my dream? Nothing! Remember, it is small hinges that open big doors!

I have also made a commitment to help others reach their financial goals. I want to work and mentor people to success. If this is something that you would be interested in learning more about, then send me an email at teamenvy@yahoo.com.

What is your dream? What burns inside of you, waiting to be accomplished? It doesn't matter what it is, if it makes you happy. Don't let anyone else determine your future. Set that goal, reach it, and let nothing stop you along the way!

Invictus
By William Ernest Henley

Out of the night that covers me,
Black as the pit from pole to pole,
I thank whatever gods may be
For my unconquerable soul.

In the fell clutch of circumstance
I have not winced nor cried aloud.
Under the bludgeoning's of chance
My head is bloody, but unbowed.

Beyond this place of wrath and tears
Looms but the Horror of the shade,
And yet the menace of the years
Finds and shall find me unafraid.

It matters not how strait the gate,
How charged with punishments the scroll,
I am the master of my fate,
I am the captain of my soul.

CHAPTER 6

*"She Lives a Life She Didn't Choose
and It Hurts Like a Pair
of New Shoes."*

—Sade

C AN I BE HONEST WITH you? This is the chapter that I didn't want to write. I don't even want to think about it anymore. Why? Because it is about real-life nightmares, haters, and dream killers. Those people who want to take everything precious in your life and stomp it on the ground while you watch. They want you to feel helpless to do anything about it. The truth is you aren't defenseless. You are powerful beyond measure and it is time for others to know it.

I spent years listening to lies and believing that I wasn't worthy, but no more. There is nothing that will stop me from becoming the most successful person I can be. Nothing ever will again. I am committed to creating my very best future and life possible.

That's why I dreaded it when I reviewed my outline and saw what chapter I had down next. I created the outline, and I knew it was there. When I wrote it down months ago it seemed right, but I have grown since then.

I have had to deal with people who didn't want me to write this book. People who ridiculed me for wanting to share my message with the world. They tried to discourage me. Another woman had commented, "I was in the Army and fought in a war and I don't feel the need to write a book in a look at me attempt!" I remember thinking, Wow, who made her feel so unworthy and without a voice? When obstacles came my way, they pointed to them as evidence and said, "See, we were right. You aren't meant to be an author!" Well, guess what? I AM. I am an author and you are the proof.

So, as reluctant as I felt about writing this chapter, I knew that I had to do so. Even though these impossibly tough life situations don't have influence in my everyday life, you may be dealing with them in *your* life. If you want to live your destiny, then you need to learn how to deal with them effectively.

You have to be able to search for the highest good in even the most tragic and horrific of things. You must constantly ask the question, "Ok, how is this possibly for my highest and best good? How is this setting me up for what I asked for or to be the person I am destined by my Creator to be!"

The same Creator who made the galaxy, the mountains, and everything beyond our true comprehension thought of you and said the world needs one of you. Then he made you so one of a kind that even your own child is only half a replication of you. So there is never going to be another you. What are you destined to do? Here is how I made the best of even the worst of moments in my life. I hope it provides the right person with the strength to overcome.

Once upon a time, which feels like a million years ago, I was deeply in love and in an abusive relationship that left me temporarily blind in the hospital.

A good-looking single guy with no children, a house, Lincoln, boat, garden, a family request for grandchildren, and a last name that ended in a vowel, oh my! The devil doesn't come dressed in a red cape and pointy horns. He comes as everything you have ever wished for!

Thank God for unanswered prayers. From our greatest tragedy comes the set up for our greatest victory.

What a shame to have sight but no true vision. How many of us are love blind? We put up with things that we couldn't bear repeating but instead bury them into the ground as our painful secret. (He hit me last night. He hit me, AGAIN, last night.) Into the ground, deep it goes, and with it a piece of our soul dies an early death.

The last blow was the last nail in the coffin and would change everything in my life forever. I could never be the same again.

It was the weekend before Thanksgiving, the start of the miracle season. Jack (my ex-boyfriend) and I had gone out window shopping at the mall. He had excitingly stopped at the Guitar Center music store, where he had fallen in love with a very expensive drum set.

We had returned home empty handed and were arguing about him wanting to use the last of his extra cash on hand to purchase the drum set this close to Christmas. I was angry that he was going to be so selfish and that he wouldn't have any money to purchase gifts for his niece and nephews. How could he think to ruin their Christmas, their favorite Uncle coming to Christmas empty handed for them because he as an adult, and selfishly wanted a new toy?

I was in the kitchen and he was standing in the dining room. I wasn't looking at him directly, which is why I didn't at first even know I had been hit. Plus, I went into shock.

I remember looking at his face as the look of terror, horror, fear, and shock slowly overtook his face. Maybe time had paused at that moment or because shock had taken over, my memory has crystalized that moment as frozen in time. I remember taking the time to mentally compute his face change. I knew something massive had occurred that I wasn't aware of.

His verbal attack had stopped, the shock had paralyzed him, and the world was still.

Carrie

Then the drip began. I looked down towards the floor and blood was gushing to it from my head. I ran to the bathroom and looked in the mirror. I was looking back at my real-life nightmare. Something straight out of a horror movie.

My eyelid was slit, and my left eye area was mangled. It looked like my eye was flipped inside out. I screamed! I remember the phone ringing and it was his sister. I answered and screamed at her. She hung up and called his parents to come over right away as they lived in the same neighborhood. When they arrived, they knew I needed to be in the hospital. I will never forget how Jack had the nerve to complain that I was getting blood on the floor.

His mother and I ended up jumping in her car to get to the hospital while his father forced Jack to go with him. On the way to the hospital, I thought up a lie (or two). I would tell my parents I had gotten in a car accident with a girlfriend in her car. I would tell the hospital that a bucket on the top shelf of a shelf in our garage had fallen on my head. I didn't want him to go to jail and become homeless on top of this nightmare with no boyfriend or anywhere to go.

How many scars do we justify because we loved the person holding the knife?

It was a few hours until the emergency room plastic surgeon on call arrived. As he examined and sewed my eye lid closed on the left side of my bed, Jack sat silently on the other side.

I remember him asking, "Why is your boyfriend so quiet?" It felt like a knife cutting into my soul. It felt like salt on a wound, insult to injury. He had not bought my lie and he knew that somewhere there was a horrible truth. I do not remember if I answered any part of that question, but Jack remained silent. He sewed me up and scheduled my emergency plastic surgery for that Wednesday, the day before the American Thanksgiving holiday.

RaNae Envy

Jack and I arrived at the hospital the morning of the surgery. I have no recollection after that until I was being wheeled out of surgery back to my room. The surgery itself consisted of my broken left orbital socket (eyebrow bone) being repaired with a Titanium metal plate and screws, then being sewn back up.

Because of the position of the injury to bandage me up post-surgery, there was a gauze blindfold that wrapped across both my eyes and around my head. Visions and memories of Metallica's One music video and lyrics filled my head.

"Darkness imprisoning me
All that I see
Absolute horror
I cannot live
I cannot die
Trapped in myself
Body my holding cell

Landmine has taken my sight
Taken my speech
Taken my hearing
Taken my arms
Taken my legs
Taken my soul
Left me with life in hell"

—Written By Lars Ulrich & James Hetfield

Returning to my cold hospital room blindfolded, not able to see anything around me, but with the knowledge that I made it out of surgery. As soon as I made it to my room, Jack put my purse on my stomach. He told me he had waited until I got out of surgery to give me my purse and that he had to go to work on an afternoon schedule. I pleaded with him, "What? Don't go to work today! Please! Please don't leave me, don't leave me here! Please, Jack!" I could not see him leave. I just became engulfed in the silence and bitter cold of the empty hospital room.

I waited for hours. Finally, I knew it was around midnight. Jack should have been off work and he had not returned. With the blindfold shifted off my good right eye, I dialed our home phone only to find out Jack was having a party at the house. He was showing off his new drum set to his buddies and drinking, while I lay temporarily blind in the hospital.

After returning home on Thanksgiving Day, I was battling with the notion of how I could let a man take away my beauty. My father had come over to see me after I got home from the hospital. The left side of my face was so swollen and black and purple that all he said was, "HOLY SHIT!" I can't imagine what Jack was thinking hearing my father's response.

I was praying the scar wouldn't leave me deformed for life. I wondered how bad it would end up looking. How would it heal? How could I, at this young age of 25, lose my beauty? Was this my karma from a previous relationship? Was I supposed to stay with the man who took my virginity? Was I going to lose my vision in that eye?

The Christmas holiday was fast approaching and the boyfriend, myself, and my father all worked in the auto industry, which completely shuts down for the holiday and new year for approximately 2 weeks.

My father had a rental property in Arizona that needed some remodeling done. My boyfriend was very handy and had done remodeling, so my father asked that we both go with him to Phoenix, Arizona. He would pay for our flights and pay Jack to help him with remodeling his rental.

It had been roughly three weeks since post-surgery. I was so happy that it had healed nicely enough that when we went to Arizona, my story about getting into a car accident would go undetected as a lie.

On the second night we were in Arizona, we went to the casino out in the desert. Jack, Dad, Uncle Tom, Uncle Steve, a girlfriend, and I were all piled up in a Grand Marquis driving home when Uncle Steve recognized a thief walking down the street. The individual had stolen thousands of dollars in guns from my Uncle Chris, who was not with us at the time.

Uncle Steve said, "That's so and so, he stole from Chris." He flipped the car around and they all, except for Jack and the girlfriend, got out and jumped the guy. I also got out of the car to distance myself from Jack.

Later that week, when Jack started an argument at the place we were staying and no one was around, I said to him, "Don't you dare touch me. If my family did that to a thief, imagine what they would do to you!" It felt good to stand up for myself.

Then on the day before we were to leave, my father told Jack and myself that he was going to take us for a drive out to Tortilla Flats and the Dam in his brother's old 1957 Ford 100!

Tortilla Flats can be reached by vehicles on State Route 88, via Apache Junction. Originally a camping ground for the prospectors who searched for gold in the Superstition Mountains in the mid-to-late 19th century, Tortilla Flats was later a freight camp for the construction of the Theodore Roosevelt Dam.

Tortilla Flats has a population of six. Once you get to the Flats, the road becomes a small, narrow, one lane dirt path winding around the mountains, taking you to the Dam. The road leading to the Dam is not often traveled. It was starting to get dark and Dad wanted to get there as fast as he could before we ran out of daylight.

The drive was unnerving for anyone. The trail winds steeply through 40 miles of rugged desert mountains, past deep reservoir lakes, like Canyon Lake and Apache Lake. There are steep cliff drops and little in the way of safety barriers. The trail requires caution when driving and it is not recommended for large RVs, SUVs, or caravans.

The drive was scary, especially for a man who had terribly and grossly abused another man's only daughter. For Jack, I am sure he wondered if my dad knew. My dad has a tough guy persona. After the events of the week, I'm sure Jack had to be wondering if he was going to kill him out in the middle of nowhere or just leave him out there.

I'm sure there were moments he felt and probably thought he wasn't ever leaving that desert again! Heck, even I was partly wondering if we all would make it. All it would take is for the brakes to go out on this old rusted truck and no one would ever find us.

The blessing was that he never hit me again. We fought some more after that, but it was just the beginning of the end.

We had one more fight but this time it was in his favor. I was blindsided but even that ended up working out ultimately in my favor.

This time I had come home, and the entire house was dark. Jack and two of his friends had been inside waiting for me in the dark. One had a Red Mustang convertible and the other friend owned a Ford Bronco, but neither of their cars were there so that I would not be alerted.

I remember yelling, "Ah, ya got your boys with you! Did he tell you he broke my face? Are you backing this creep, really?"

I ran to the kitchen and grabbed the blender to use it as a weapon. It was three men on one. I just started swinging. Go ahead, come near me, I dare you! At this moment, I had so much built up anger and resentment inside of me for what he had done, I could have fought the world!

Their goal was to antagonize a fight with me, while one of them called the police. Then the three of them would keep the fight going with me long enough for the cops to show up. The goal was that I would be sent to jail as a mad woman!

It worked. I spent the weekend in the county jail until a video arraignment with a woman judge. Jack appeared in court wearing an arm sling and played the victim until the judge asked, "What would make you attack him?"

I responded, "Your honor, did he happen to tell you that he broke my eye socket in November and left me blind in the hospital and that I had to have plastic surgery?"

She turned to him with a look of disgust and asked him, "Is this true?"

He only had the guts to nod his answer.

The truth shall set you free. The judge reduced my charges from domestic violence to disorderly conduct and ordered anger management.

I had secretly saved up money by this point. Now I went and bought my own house. Jack and I had plans to build a beautiful custom home, but I ended up buying a complete fixer-upper. I remember thinking, I'd rather be safe and happy. I don't wish him harm. I just want him away from me.

I would spend most of my time not dating, but focusing on more worthwhile activities and travelling.

"Sometimes a change of perspective is all
it takes to see the light."
—*Dan Brown*

Kintsugi (golden joinery), also known as golden repair, is the Japanese art of repairing broken pottery with lacquer dusted or mixed with powdered gold, silver, or platinum. It is a method similar to the *maki-e* technique. As a philosophy, it treats breakage and repair as part of the history of an object, rather than something to disguise. As a philosophy, kintsugi can be seen to have similarities to the Japanese philosophy of wabi-sabi, an embracing of the flawed or imperfect.

Kintsugi can also relate to the Japanese philosophy of mushin or "no mind", which encompasses the concepts of non-attachment, acceptance of change, and fate as aspects of human life. Not only is there no attempt to hide the damage, but the repair is literally illuminated, a kind of physical expression of the spirit of mushin. It carries connotations of fully existing within the moment, of non-attachment, and of equanimity amid changing conditions.

"The best revenge is massive success."
—Frank Sinatra

As I healed physically and mentally, there was nothing left to do but learn and grow. I was going to make sure that I became a massive success. Knowledge is something that once obtained, no man on Earth could ever take away from you. Paper they may rip into a million pieces, but they could never pry into your brain and retrieve or remove an idea. Beauty inevitably will fade, but knowledge will grow to become the strongest of your shields of protection.

I like to think this is where I received my super powers for being a visionary. I was temporarily blind, but I was given a golden repair. Where others have to see it to believe it, I sometimes see it and then reality forces me to believe it.

Patch Adams

It's funny how you will be tested on what you believe. There is no testimony without a test. This morning, as I was getting ready to work on this chapter, a hater showed up on Facebook. I had posted an article about how the owner of Amazon.com had briefly had the distinction of being The Richest Man in the World and the power of online shopping. This hater wrote in the comments, "You are obsessed with being rich." At first, I was tempted to let the negative message bring me down or try to argue with her—but something rose up inside of me and inspired me to be more.

My company does amazing things. We have more products than most online stores, and we pay our customers to shop. Three years ago, we got Shop.com groceries. We are a company powered by the people, for the people. We take the money spent by other companies to advertise and we reinvest it back into our shoppers, giving them an opportunity to share in our success.

Here is what I believe: no one has the right to tell what you can and cannot achieve in life. I was created by God/Creator to do remarkable things. Nothing anyone says or does will stop me. I am obsessed with personal freedom, and that is what I help people to achieve. I don't want to see others work a job that they hate for 40 years only to retire and die. That is not what life should be.

I love listening to what Tyrese Gibbons says:

"Only those who can see the invisible can do what is impossible."

Your vision of reaching your goals and dreams is something that very few people can see. It is important that you remember that.

The Usual Suspects

So, how can you tell when someone is trying to steal your dreams and your future? Good question. How can you fight something when you don't even know that it is happening? Ask yourself if you are experiencing any of these situations to know for sure.

1. You Feel Deflated

When you are around Dream Stealers, you feel flat. You feel like nothing good is possible in life. Before you hung around with them, you were happy and you knew that life is good. After a few minutes with them, you are left feeling like an empty balloon, deflated. You can feel it hit you like a ton of bricks.

2. Dream Stealers Are Always Negative

Do you know someone that can turn the best things in life into a negative? It doesn't matter what you say, they will find some way to make it bad. These types of people never have any hope and they want to make sure you don't either. Be careful not to fall into the habit of negativity!

3. They Are Jealous of You

These types of people will start out by acting nice to you and getting close to you. They may be overly friendly and seem very interested in who you are and what you are doing. You will notice that they aren't actually helping you. They will take the information they acquire and find a way to use it against you, often with the intent of stopping you from moving forward while making themselves look good.

4. They Make Problems Bigger Than What They Are

When you mention any type of problem you are having, Dream Stealers will take advantage of it. They will blow it up so big that you end up agreeing with them and quitting. The obstacles start to appear so enormous that you feel they are insurmountable.

5. They Express Their 'Concerns' About What You Are Doing

This is an especially deceitful tactic. They come to you and want to "warn you" about what you are doing and how it can ruin your life. They appear to care but the whole time they are speaking, you know that their concerns aren't motivated by loving concern.

So, what is the main motivation with these people? You are doing something they have barely dreamed of doing. You threaten their comfort zone. They have convinced themselves that the "average person" cannot succeed. When you, an "average person", does succeed, it blows away their excuses and shows them who they really are. As long as no one else becomes successful, Dream Stealers can hide in the crowd and be content with a mediocre life. As soon as you start to rise above, they feel threatened and want to bring you back down to their "safe" level.

Against All Odds Again

You are going to run into negative people who want to steal your dreams. It is going to happen, so you shouldn't be surprised when it does. It is a test of your resolve, to see if you are worthy of the goal you set for yourself. If you can't pass that test, you will never move forward. Some days you will be tested at every step.

Currently by law in Carmel, Calif., any woman who wishes to traipse through the streets rocking shoes over two inches high with less than one square inch of heel surface area must pick up a permit from City Hall. Oddly specific, you say? It's a liability issue. The permits, which are free, relieve Carmel, "from any and all liability for damages to her/himself or to others caused by her/his falling upon the public streets or sidewalks of the City while wearing such shoes." You are all living dangerously, ladies.

How do you pass the test? Here are some ways to deal with those people who try to steal your joy. First, determine in your heart that it doesn't matter what they say, you are going to move forward. You made the commitment to your dream. You will continue despite what they say.

Second, don't argue with them. Every time you argue, you give them power over you. If you do, it legitimizes their behavior and gives them weapons that they can use against you. Let them say what they want, you don't have to internalize it and you don't have act on it. Third, remember that your worth is not based on what they say or think. You were created by God to succeed and nothing that anyone says can succeed against the will of God.

Show them that nothing will stop you. Lastly, keep your self-talk strong. What do I mean by that? It is that voice in your head, the one that tells you if you will succeed or fail. Is it the Angel or the Devil on your shoulder speaking through your thoughts? When we hear negative words, it can be tempting to repeat them in your head over and over again. When you hear negatives, tell yourself the opposite. Plant the seed of accomplishment and not doubt.

As I close this chapter, I want to share the powerful lyrics to the song *My Way,* made famous by the legendary Frank Sinatra. When the attacks come, this song gets me back on track. Find the things that center you and keep you focused on what is important.

"My Way"
I'll state my case, of which I'm certain
I've lived a life that's full
I travelled each and every highway

Yes, there were times, I'm sure you knew
When I bit off more than I could chew
But through it all, when there was doubt
I ate it up and spit it out
I faced it all and I stood tall and did it my way

To say the things, he truly feels and
not the words of one who kneels
The record shows I took the blows and did it my way

CHAPTER 7

"You Don't Have To Be Great To Start, But You Have To Start To Be Great."

—Zig Ziglar

L EAH SAT STARING AT HER computer screen. If you looked at her, you would have thought that she was fine. However, on the inside, she was paralyzed with fear. "Why can't I do this?" she asked herself over and over.

All the other representatives in her company didn't seem to have a problem talking to people about joining their businesses. Yet she couldn't even type a simple sentence on Social Media about what she did.

"What's wrong with me?" For the next ½ hour, she reminded herself of every negative thing her father had told her. By the time she was done, the laptop lid was closed. She got up to watch TV and hopefully escape her heavy heart.

Reality Bites

This chapter is about one of biggest obstacles you face on your road to success, which is how to start. Many times, you quit before you even begin. It is time for that to stop. If you feel like your only speed is stall, then keep reading and be set free to finally move forward.

The first thing to understand is that taking that first step is one of the most important things you can do. Why? When you do, you are fulfilling a promise to yourself. Whether you realize it or not, your desire to live a successful life is a gift from God. When you first felt it, you knew that it had to be done. In a sense, you promised yourself that you would make it. Every time you didn't start, it drives you one step further away from ever reaching that goal.

What is the biggest reason we don't start? Fear. Fear of failure, fear of success, fear of what people will think, and the list goes on and on. Now we covered a lot about fear in Chapter 4, so I am not going to go over it all again, but this is what I do want to stress. Most fear we have in business is irrational, meaning that there is nothing that can harm us.

Most of these fears are ingrained in us during childhood. Like my mother saying my whole life, "Don't roller skate, don't rollerblade, you will break your leg." You know what? I roller skated and roller bladed, and I never broke my leg. The fear that she tried to instill into me is that you don't try anything new or risky because you will get hurt, which is a lie.

When you feel this way, you need to dig deep and examine why. What subconscious messages are hindering you from success? Once you find them, you can address them and overcome your fear. You can make the choice to move past the fear and act. You can become the person you have always wanted to be.

Facing The Giants

One thing that I love about the movie *Facing the Giants* is how the coach worked on his team's mindset, especially how they saw themselves. Over the course of year, he turned a losing team into champions. When you work on your mindset, it is the one change that will truly bring you success.

I like to explain it as becoming bulletproof. There is nothing from the outside that can affect you and nothing that stops you from the inside can get out. You become unstoppable when you can withstand all exterior influences and overcome the negative inner ones.

In order to become successful, you have to be willing to be mocked, ridiculed, made fun of, and called names. You have to be bulletproof, knowing that your path is your path and where you are going is good.

Here is one thing I have learned: when everything seems to be going against you, that is a sign that you are on the right road. Success will test you to see if you worthy.

How do you become bulletproof in your mindset? The first thing to recognize is that this is a process. You don't make it overnight. It is something that you work on for a period of time.

Second, you want to immerse yourself in the teachings of others who have been successful and can teach you how to follow that journey. People, like Jim Rohn, Zig Ziglar, Raymond

Aaron and Tony Robbins, have all been where you are at and can show you a better way.

Third, you may have to limit the time you spend with certain people. There will be people in your life, who don't want you to succeed. It's not that they want you to fail, but as you move forward, it shows them what they are missing out on and are afraid to go after, so they try to stop you.

Small Changes Make Big Differences

How do you eat an elephant? One bite at a time. There are a lot of mediocre people going above and beyond mediocre but making it look extraordinary by putting in that little bit extra. It's that little bit extra that makes them rise above the crowd. It makes them look like they are doing more, but anyone can do that. If you want it, then you can accomplish it. Nobody is that different.

Everyone can be successful. Some of the most successful people have dropped out of high school or college. They aren't the smartest or the fastest. Look at people like Oprah, who struggled, had everything going against her, and yet she made it. My point is you don't even have to be the most successful. You just have to be the one that shows up.

I love what Oprah says in this video on YouTube https://www.youtube.com/watch?v=sQQavHyHtBg, where she talks about a painting she has hanging in her house. The name of that painting is called *To the Highest Bidder 1906*. *To The Highest Bidder* is a pre-Civil War scene depicting a mother and daughter about to be separated in a slave auction. African-American artist **Harry Herman Roseland** noted that this is a sad commentary on the life of slaves.

In her library, Oprah has a framed list of enslaved African-American people. The list is of Negros and other livestock that are being sold and the prices for affixed to them. Each one is a reminder of how far she has come and how much farther she has yet to go because of them.

Sometimes Oprah stops and reads the list out loud so that she is reminded of the absurdity of the prices placed on each one.

Jonas $500

Sarah $900

Elizabeth $800

Now I want you to come to a new realization, that slavery was never abolished. It was only changed to include everyone. The only difference was a couple of zeros.

Jonas now makes $50,000, Sarah makes $90,000, and Elizabeth makes $80,000. They get to live in their own homes and stay home on the weekends. To the highest bidder, we have become a society chained to the dollar or other currency, letting it control when we wake up, eat, sleep, and see our loved ones.

RaNae Envy

How much did they pay you to give up on your dreams?

Her ancestors paid the price, so she could be who she is now. There were those in your past who paid the price so that you can live up to your full potential. Have you ever thought about that? They did what they did so that their children, grandchildren, and great grandchildren could live the life they wanted.

When you think about that, it makes you see how small you are living and how much more you could be doing. In the video, Oprah quoted Maya Angelou, saying, "I come as one, but I stand as 10,000." She then adds, "I stand not only as 10,000 to the tenth power, I stand on solid rock. I stand because I am the dream and the hope of the slave. I am more than the seed of the free that Langston Hughes talked about in the poem *The Negro Mother*. I am the fruit. I am the flower. I am the blossoming tree and I shall not be moved."

Want to know about a small change that will propel you beyond mediocrity? Think about those in your past who paid a big price. What are you going to do, to make life for your future generations even better? In the auto industry, it was the past Union leaders that fought for the next generation to have a little more and then a little more.

Think about your ancestors who immigrated to new countries so that you could have a better life. Think about those who fought in the World Wars, so that you could be free. Think about the sacrifices of those who have gone before. When you think of that, it changes how you see yourself. It encourages you to be and become more.

Small changes in thinking can lead to big results in your life. Once you start to make those incremental changes, you will start to notice those negative thoughts and will be able to replace them with positive, strengthening thoughts that move you towards success.

My Story

My life has changed so much since I worked on my mindset. Let's start with my current boyfriend. I would write letters to God. It was a way for me to declare what I was looking for and trust that it was going to come. So, I would write, "Dear God, please send me a man that I can admire, that I can look up to. He must be really strong, and really tough, in fact the strongest, toughest guy on the planet and he has to be at least six-foot-tall. LOL"

I have this picture in my mind of the man that I want. The man that I can become part of a power couple with. A man who shares my dreams and will work with me to achieve them. Those are the things I wrote in my letter to God and He has an amazing way of answering.

An opportunity opened for me to get a part-time job at the airport. I always knew that I wanted to work for an airline at least once before I die, it was a bucket list item. That is where

I met my boyfriend. He is like a knight in shining armor at this job and treats me like a princess. It wasn't long before I realized that HE was the one. You know my request for the strongest and toughest man on the face of the earth? He is very strong and tough and tall, over 6 feet like I asked.

The same thing happened when I took my first Neuro-Linguistic Programming class. The instructor said, "Why aren't you living your dream to go live out west?" My response was, "I own my house. I just can't get rid of my house." He suggested that I rent it out and all I could was come up with were more excuses as to why I couldn't. He challenged me to think differently about it and I couldn't get it out of my head.

Within five days, someone came up to me and said, "RaNae, I don't even know why I am asking you this, but do you know anyone who has a house for rent? It has to be a ranch. It has to be at least two bedrooms, and it has to be at this price point." It was the exact cost of my mortgage, and my house is an all-brick ranch, and it's three-bedroom, not two. My dream of living out west was one step closer.

When you start paying attention to your mindset, realizing that you are the captain of your destiny, then you can learn how to control your thoughts and not just let them run wild. You can move mountains with your faith in God's promises to us. He gave us this power and freedom, but also our free will. Those, who choose to really learn how to drive and even play nice with their own minds, are the ones that rise above anything.

Floating

One thing that has been so helpful to me is float therapy. In ten inches of water heated to your body temperature, with 800 pounds of Epsom salt in the tank. You go in the tank and it automatically makes you float. Shut the door and float for like an hour or two, depending on where you go.

It is sensory deprivation, so there is no sound or light. You are in darkness. You are floating in this water that is the same temperature as your skin. The water starts to not be as apparent, and it becomes forced meditation. It is an experience that you never had before, as your mind becomes limitless. It frees you from the external things, so you can get down to the true you.

It's the closest thing, in my opinion, to being back in the womb. You are in darkness, so you can't see anything or hear anything. Not only that, a baby has a perfect mind. Floating helps you get back to your core self. With each session, it is like you are doing more and more personal work. Even for someone who is a complete water baby, like myself, when you first get in, before you can get comfortable, you also have to face a fear.

Here is what I want to leave you with. This is your time to shine. It is your time to become the person you know you can be and to succeed, not just in business, but in life as well. I would love to help you. Connect with me at The Envy Factor on Facebook. Let's see how we can work together to help you become the best you possible.

CHAPTER 8

"All That I Am, Or Hope To Be, I Owe To My Angel Mother."

—*Abraham Lincoln*

MOTHERS ARE OUR FIRST HOME. They are the first heart we hear beating. As a matter of fact, children are the first person to hear a mother's heartbeat from the inside. God/Creator thought so highly of women that he gave them the most important job ever, to make all the people and to be an expression of the closest thing to God's true unconditional love.

I loved my mother deeply. She struggled all the years I knew her and yet she always loved me. In this chapter, I want to share with you the circumstances surrounding her death in the hopes that no one will have to go through what I did.

I was working midnights in the Engine Plant at this time. It was about 3 in the morning, December 3, 2015. I was working like normal, driving equipment to deliver parts throughout the plant. It was a highly physical job that had you racing all over the place. It was fast paced, but you earned longer breaks because you were not tied to the line.

That day, I became unsettled and wanted to be left alone. Have you ever had the feeling that something very important is happening to someone you love but you don't know what it is? That was me. Something was up but I couldn't put my finger on it. After a while, I shook it off, went home after my shift and slept like normal.

When I woke up, I had a text message from my aunt. When I called her, she was screaming. I could not understand any of the words she had said. I remember saying to her, "I don't know what you are trying to say but I think you are trying to tell me my mom is dead."

"Yes! Get here right away!"

I showed up to my mother's apartment and there was my 85-year-old grandmother, crying out to God, "I just lost my best friend! What am I going to do? I just lost my best friend!"

Then they wheeled her out on a gurney, in a thick green body bag. I remember feeling so disconnected from the idea of that bag being my mother. I was in total disbelief. I dreaded having to go tell my brother and call my father.

Later that evening, my aunt had my brother and I go back to my mother's apartment to get her personal belongings. The horror of it engulfed my mind.

There was blood and pills on the living room floor in front of the couch and two distinct puddles of blood next to the sink in the kitchen. I remember trying to wrap my mind around the horror. I thought, this had to have been a murder. Someone had to have broken in and done this to her. There is no way someone could do this to themselves.

Suicide Squad

I spent the next few nights with my girlfriend, Jacque, crying my eyes out and trying to understand it all. Even worse, nightmares consumed my sleep. Visions of my mother sitting on a couch in the dark with knives shredding her lower abdomen and laughing like a maniacal clown or joker while doing the unthinkable! I was so deep into my dreams that I could not control or stop it. I could only go through it.

Jacque told me that I was moaning and yelling in my sleep and that it was painful and heartbreaking for her to even watch.

For the first time, I completely understood what it was like for HER (my mother), when her father committed suicide. That hurt even more. Knowing how it felt and how it can destroy you, how could she do this to me and my brother?

All the positive and strong mental work I had done my whole life to try and prevent being depressed like my mom, and instead, she gave me her disease. There was nothing I could do except fight the demons in my sleep and know that God will somehow turn this tragedy into a testimony and triumph one day!

I had the thoughts that everyone does when a family member committed suicide, "What could I have done to save her? I should have done more. I should not have worked so much."

My best friend since my parent's divorce saved my life. She stopped me and said, "Don't say that! You could have been with her 24/7 and the moment you stepped away, she would have done it!! There was nothing you could have done to stop her!"

Talk about adding insult to injury! Not only was I facing having to bury my mom for Christmas, I was also left with most of the financial burden of the cost of the funeral.

She had left instructions for all the arrangements she had made. What she wanted to be buried in was hanging in the spare closet. When my aunt went to the closet and saw the clothes, there was the Christmas present I had given her the Christmas before, a beautiful purple cape. Oh, the heart break of it all, having to bury Mom in the Christmas present I had bought her. I had been thinking about how this year I was going to get her another one, just in a different color.

Inception

My aunt and I had made an appointment at the funeral home that had sent the ambulance to the scene. They gave me a card over her body bag.

We had sat down and discussed things, like prayer cards and more. The funeral home manager said to me, "I have to go work up this estimate real quick and tell you the cost."

I said to him, "Can't you give me an idea of how much it will cost, so I even have a clue, because I have never paid for a funeral!"

He responded very cockily, "Oh I'm going to knock your socks off!"

I responded, "Excuse me, you are going to knock MY socks off?!"

At this point, I went from a grieving daughter to a woman on a mission. The term itself means to take someone by surprise or to hit someone so hard that their socks would fall off! How could someone be so callous at a time like this?

In the movie *The Inception*, Leonardo DiCaprio goes into a shared dreaming to incept an idea into someone's mind. When they were deep into the dream, an outside partner would give them a kick to wake them up.

When he said to a grieving woman who had just tragically lost her mother that he was going to "knock my socks off", he gave me the kick that brought me out of my real-life nightmare and into the realm of what is in my power to accomplish.

If you are going through hell, look for your kick and regain your power.

I went to my father and brother and told them what they had said at the funeral home. They wanted just $1,500 to drive her body from the morgue to the cemetery, to which my father heartlessly responded, "She won't fit in your car?" As if to insinuate that I would pick up my mother's body to be frugal!

The thought sent my brother into a rage towards my father and he threatened to kill him in the heat of the moment.

Could my personal nightmare have become any worse? To tell you the truth, this whole nightmare had made me feel completely alone for the first time in my life!

The day of the funeral, I had chosen to read Og Mandino's Scroll #2, from *The Greatest Salesman In the World*. It gave me strength and it reversed what I had found in my mother's last writings where she wrote, "I hate the cold. I hate the winter. I hate the rain!" The scroll talks about loving all things and you will become born again.

It says, love the sun for it warms your bones and the rain because it will cleanse your spirit. That the light shows you the way, yet without darkness we wouldn't be able to see the beautiful stars. That we encounter sadness to open our souls. When you are moved to praise, shout it from the roofs and sing like the birds do for their Creator!

I will greet this day with love in my heart. And how will I act? I will love all manners of men for each has qualities to be admired even though they be hidden. With love I will tear down the wall of suspicion and hate which they have built round their hearts and in its place will I build bridges so that my love may enter their souls. I will love the ambitious for they can inspire me; I will love the failures for they can teach me. I will love the kings for they are but

*human; I will love the meek for they are divine. I will love
the rich for they are yet lonely; I will love the poor for they
are so many. I will love the young for the faith they hold;
I will love the old for the wisdom they share. I will love the
beautiful for their eyes of sadness; I will love the ugly for
their souls of peace.*

I will greet this day with love in my heart.

It took me three years to begin to fully understand why and how she did it. I comforted myself by thinking she just planned and went on the best vacation. How could I blame her for not wanting a life that had no fun, travel, or much of anything to look forward to? She used to always want to travel more but her health wasn't good enough. This way, at least she gets to come along with me everywhere I go. Oh, the places I am going to show you, Mom!

Her little note left to me was, "RaNae, thank you for being my beautiful daughter. I love you! Please still love me! I will be watching over you and I will be able to help you (with your dreams!)"

After a few months, I just could not shake the uneasy feeling inside. I went to my family practice doctor. The first thing I said to him was, "I have never been this weak before in my life!" He assured me that I was not being weak, just grieving. He had just lost his father and understood what I was going through. He prescribed some medication to help my mental state. I took them for four months but went off them because they numbed out my emotions, my drive, my edge, and my ambition.

Suicide is one of the most heart-breaking things you can go through in life. There are so many questions that will never be answered, and the guilt will eat you up if you allow it to.

I choose life and to release the guilt. There was nothing I could do to stop her. This was no spur of the moment, she had planned it and picked the time to carry it out. Even if I had stopped her that night, she would have done it at the next available opportunity. She had struggled with depression and mental illness for so long, that nothing would have helped. I have to accept that and do everything I can to make her proud as she watches down from heaven.

If you or someone you love is dealing with thoughts of suicide, please get help. Call your local suicide prevention line or mental health center. Don't wait until it is too late. There are professionals trained to help you.

The Secret Garden

Adam and Eve lived in Eden. It is not a place anywhere on the map, unlike Jerusalem. Eden is defined as paradise. Eden is the garden, where according to the account in Genesis, Adam and Eve first lived. Eden is a place of pristine or abundant natural beauty that they were to cultivate and grow.

Eden can be and is intended to be created by man and woman here on Earth. No different than you tending to your home and garden.

Do you know what happens if you don't tend to and take care of your garden? Well, it will become so overrun with weeds that you won't bear any fruit, let alone grow anything in abundance. No one is impressed with a weed garden. It is missing order and not in earthly harmony. No different than abandoning your garden.

What does the garden represent in your life? It is your spouse, kids, family, and friends. They need to be taken care of like a garden and you need to prepare your garden through cultivation. Let's explore the definition of cultivation.

Cultivate

    1: to prepare and use for the raising of crops.

    2: **a:** to foster the growth of plants

        b: culture in the sense of oysters for pearls

        c: to improve by labor, care, or study: REFINE *cultivate* the mind . . . *cultivated* a reputation as a hard-core wheeler-dealer

    3: further, encourage, *cultivate* the arts

    4: to seek the society of: make friends with

Men are the seed given to women and the garden of life. The seed, the fertilized ripened ovule of a flowering plant containing an embryo, is capable normally of germination to produce a new plant. A seed is also a source of development or growth. Remember, men used to study and have libraries, not man caves today.

Mother Theresa always said, "If you want to change the world, go home and love your family. We can have paradise and Heaven on Earth when we live the way we were intended."

"A woman's highest calling is to lead a man to his soul,
so as to unite him with Source. Her lowest calling is to
seduce, separating man from his soul and leave him
aimlessly wandering. A man's highest calling is to protect
woman, so she is free to walk the earth unharmed.
Man's lowest calling is to ambush and
force his way into the life of a woman."
—Cherokee Proverb

We were meant to live better than we have been. However, what I see happening is men and women are not living in harmony and creating a safe loving environment for the garden or the seeds.

Remember the kinetic balls at the beginning of the book. That is what most people's lives are like. Men and women smack each other back and forth and the kids get hit from both sides in the middle. How are children supposed to learn love when they don't see it at home? Single parents are showing children to live without love and to struggle.

We were not meant to raise children in a one parent home. We were meant to learn love at home and from there we contribute the best of ourselves to society. Happy, loving children are our gift to the world and our responsibility. As women, we need to choose our seed more carefully.

There is a power struggle. The women want to be valued for their opinion and intellect and the men do not know how to deal with this new modern-day woman. I believe the ones who seek higher understanding are living with the most harmony.

There is discord among all races in the world right now. The root cause is not knowing how to fully love and support each other. It all starts with the union of man and woman, and that unity has been destroyed in this day and age.

Single women have become the new normal head of the house. When there is no one to protect the women and children, the devil runs rampant. During the end of time, the Bible says that wickedness and evil will run rampant all over the world. It is happening. History repeats itself until it is rewritten.

As a woman, you have an incredible power to create life. It is a special gift that translates into every other area, including business. Don't be afraid to allow that creative, wonderful, giving side out. It is what makes you special and your contributions to the world amazing.

In the next chapter, I want to share with you an aspect that we all face as women and that is injustice. What do you do when you are trying to live your dream and the attacks come?

CHAPTER 9

"Injustice Anywhere Is A Threat To Justice Everywhere."

—Martin Luther King Jr

HAVE TO WARN YOU THIS chapter is not for the faint of heart. I will be sharing my story of being unjustly confined and the story of others who were misunderstood and persecuted for it.

I wish that I didn't have to write this chapter, but what I am about to tell you is the truth. You need to be aware, so if it happens to you, then you know how to deal with it.

This is the next level above dealing with obstacles and people who are trying to discourage you from your dream. This is when the world's systems try to violently and forcefully destroy your dreams all together.

It was September 22, 2018 and I had just finished writing this book (or so I had thought). I was listening to Les Brown and how he described being adopted and how he felt unloved growing up. Then one day, someone changed his perspective and told him his adopted mother loved him very much and chose him out of the whole world. That stopped that no good, stinking thinking, which replayed in his mind, of not feeling worthy of love.

It got me thinking about my mother and deep down I thought, "Did my mother really never want to see me again?"

Then a revelation came to me about the way my mother killed herself. Out of respect for her, I won't share all the gory details. In that moment, God showed me something that allowed my heart to heal from that thought. My soul was renewed. I knew God/Creator's love was true and He truly has our greatest victory in mind. I felt a happiness that I hadn't experienced in a long time. I felt like celebrating and doing something a little outrageous. My faith was restored, and I wanted to shout it out from the mountain tops so the world could hear it and know the truth.

Bruce Almighty

It is 6 am and I am compelled to do something! Something big, but not too big. I get all dressed up. I put one of my Desigual dresses on. I put on ALL my nice jewellery, including my big fat round diamond ring and my tiara with my birthstone in it, which my Aunt had bought me for a birthday present. Then I go to Starbucks! Why shouldn't the world see me at my best?

As I'm driving, I imagine the wonderful things I would love to have happen in my life, like what it would be like to have a parade in my honor.

Since no one is on the road, I made a calculated risk and decided to drive on the opposite side of the road. It was so freeing, conquering my fear and doing what I never had the guts to do before. I get to the street the coffee shop is on and drove around the building. Once I got my coffee, I see a police officer in the parking lot. Since I have this new confidence, and he must be so bored sitting there at that time of the morning with nothing to do, I decide to be nice and talk to him. I pull up alongside of him in my White Mercedes Benz and say, "Hey, is there anything you want to talk about?"

He in return says, "Yeah, let's talk. I'll get behind you." He pulls his cop car behind my car. He then comes up to my car window and I ask him if he has ever seen the movie Bruce Almighty? No, he had not. Another officer shows up, I ask him the same thing. No, he hadn't either. Finally, a 3rd cop comes to the circle in front of me and I ask him, "Have you seen the movie Bruce Almighty?" He responds, "Yes, I have!"

I said, "Great, then you are the one I want to talk to." He instantly became uncomfortable as he had a lower rank than the others and was not supposed to do the talking. At that point, I didn't realize what was happening. They saw a rich, white woman, dressed to the nines and assumed there was something wrong with me.

They asked me to go to the local emergency room by ambulance. I remember thinking, "Just go with the flow darling!" Just smile and be your charming self. Tell them about your amazing book and how excited you are, and everything will be marvellous. I was oblivious and trusted that they wanted to help me.

Infinity War

They took me to the medical clinic where my primary doctor has been since I was little. My best friend from high school is the receptionist on the family practice side, so there was no need or reason for me to be alarmed in any way.

The doctor that approached me seemed mean and evil spirited. All of a sudden, I was very scared. He was talking to me about medications to help me think more rationally. I instantly said to him, "OMG, you are what is wrong with America! I don't need any medication, there is nothing wrong with me! I really did write a book." Probably not the right thing to say to a doctor who has the power to lock me up in a mental hospital, which is what they did. I had made him mad and now I was going to pay for it.

I backed up to the corner of the room so no one could attack me from behind. I told them clearly that I had written a book and I had proof, if they would just stop, but they wouldn't listen. I also made it clear that if they did anything else to me all of America would know about it. I have kept my word.

The doctor was trying to pink tag me, which means you are held against your will or in involuntary commitment for at least 72 hours for assessment and you cannot leave.

I evaded them long enough for them to call back two police officers to the hospital and help nurses and this doctor strap me down to the hospital bed by the arms and ankles. There was no way I was going without a fight. They finally got me down and on the count of 1, 2, 3, they double tranquilized me. Then they catharized me and left me tied up for hours until I regained consciousness.

They also had given me two Ativan's on top of the double Haldol (tranquilizer) They overdosed me to such a point that it took 4 hours before I was conscious enough to safely transport.

Looking back on it, there are a lot of questions I have. "What if I was black? What if I wasn't mentally strong? What if I was a white man driving a Rolls Royce and said I wrote a book? What if they would have killed me? Would anyone had known the truth or trusted that these physicians gave me appropriate care and my physical body just didn't handle it?"

Then they took me against my will to the mental hospital and kept me long enough to drain my insurance benefits. I was held against my will for five days. Even then, the doctor didn't want to release me because he said, I was STILL having grandiose thoughts because I continued to say I wrote a book.

Thank the lord, I had worn all my expensive jewellery. The cops treated me like a crazy rich chick, because I believe if I had been poor or black, I would likely have been killed or faced jail time. Instead, I was sent on a five-day vacation with prescribed drugs that had effects stronger than most illegal street drugs.

How many lives have been muted and stolen by doctors playing God!

In *Infinity War*, the Avengers unite to battle their most powerful enemy yet—the evil Thanos. On a mission, Thanos plans to use the artifacts to inflict his twisted will on reality. The fate of the planet and existence itself has never been more uncertain, as everything the Avengers have fought for has led up to this moment.

> *"I'm not looking for forgiveness, and I'm way past asking permission. Earth just lost her best defender, so we're here to fight. And if you want to stand in our way, we'll fight you too."*
> —Captain America

I later found out that in the United States today one person is involuntarily incarcerated in a psychiatric facility every 40 seconds. Perhaps a friend, family member, or neighbour, and more often than not, they will be brutally treated and force-fed mind-altering pharmaceuticals.

One person every 40 seconds equals 2,160 people per day. I hope you are sitting down because that number multiplied by 365 days of the year equals 788,400 people per year are being involuntary committed to a mental unit of a hospital. The government is giving these facilities massive amounts of money. It is a hidden prison. Hidden in plain sight.

It is a modern-day concentration camp that makes what Hitler did during the Holocaust look like it never ended. Starting in 1933, the Nazis built a network of concentration camps in Germany for political opponents and people deemed "undesirable."

The United States Holocaust Memorial Museum defines the Holocaust as the "systematic, bureaucratic, state-sponsored persecution and murder of six million Jews by the Nazi regime and its collaborators."

In disturbing similarity, Nazi human experimentation was a series of medical experiments on large numbers of prisoners, including children, by Nazi Germany in its concentration camps in the early to mid-1940s, during World War II and the Holocaust. Nazi physicians and their assistants forced prisoners into participating; they did not willingly volunteer, and no consent was given for the procedures. Typically, the experiments resulted in death, trauma, disfigurement or permanent disability, and as such are considered examples of medical torture.

Please don't get me wrong. There are people who need to be there for their own safety or the safety of others, but in the day and age of Amazon, where hundreds to thousands of average people self-publish and become authors every day, who is crazier? The person who says that they are writing a book or the people who don't believe her. If it had been 50-60 years ago, I might see where they could think I am crazy, but not in 2019.

Doctor Who

The poetic justice is, I later found out about Doctor Who. Doctor Who is a British science fiction television character, whose shows have been produced since 1963. Despite his plethora of victories, the Doctor does not like the use of guns and violence. Instead of blasting his enemies with heat vision, like Superman or taking them down with hand to hand combat, the Doctor uses other weapons, like talking, cleverness, and in this case, books.

Hint: You are the weapon!

"You want weapons? We're in a library! Books! Best weapons in the world! This room's the greatest arsenal we could have. Arm yourself!"

—*The Doctor*

Alice in Wonderland: Through the Looking Glass

Have you ever seen *Alice Through the Looking Glass*?

There is a part in the movie where Alice was knocked out and woke up in a mental ward with arms and legs strapped down. The doctor comes in saying, "Let's see. Excitable, emotional, prone to fantasy, a textbook case of female hysteria. Untreatable some say. I beg to differ."

As he pulls out an enormous syringe, she stabs the doctor with the syringe instead. He drops to the floor, allowing Alice to escape from the mental institution.

At first thought, this would seem absurd in this day and age, considering *Alice Through the Looking Glass* was written in 1871. That is until I made the discovery of how this practice is still being done on women today in 2018, by old-way thinking of medical professionals in the U.S.

It would seem easy to laugh at these anti-woman approaches to mental health as absurdly archaic—until you read the recently released statistics about psychiatric medication where 1 in 4 women are on psychotropic pharmaceutical drugs prescribed by their doctors.

Maybe Hollywood is really trying to tell us something? Hollywood always hints at current corruption that needs to be exposed! Are out dated old medical practices a deeper rooted #MeToo Movement?

At the beginning of the 20th century, psychiatry and psychology infiltrated Hollywood, redefining creativity as a form of neurosis.

One in four suggests that either women, or our doctors, are being sold on an ideal of mental health that is unrealistic. The world's mostly male 'great thinkers' have tended to say so, characterizing women as the weaker sex, both physically or psychologically.

In the 5th century BC, Hippocrates (i.e., the founder of western medicine, in what may not go down as his greatest achievement) first coined the term "hysteria"—from "hystera," or uterus—and also attributed its cause to abnormal movements of the womb in a woman's body.

Feminist social historians of both genders argue that hysteria is caused by women's oppressive social roles rather than by their bodies or psyches. They have sought its sources in cultural myths of femininity and in male domination.

Female hysteria was once a common medical diagnosis for women, a basic catch all diagnosis exclusive to women. Basically, medically deeming women crazy. Then they wonder why the women are crazy MAD and pissed off. It is no longer recognized by medical authorities as a medical disorder, but still has lasting social implications. The American Psychiatric Association dropped the term *hysteria* in 1952.

Even though it was categorized as a disease, hysteria's symptoms were synonymous with normal functioning female sexuality. Women considered to have it exhibited a wide array of symptoms, including anxiety, shortness of breath, fainting, nervousness, sexual desire, insomnia, fluid retention, heaviness in the abdomen, irritability, loss of appetite for food or sex, (paradoxically) sexually forward behaviour, and a "tendency to cause trouble for others." In extreme cases, the woman may have been forced to enter an insane asylum or to have undergone a surgical hysterectomy.

There is a worldwide system that has been discrediting women and labelling them as crazy and intellectually unstable since the beginning of time. This thought process is holding us down and has not been loving, kind, nor advantageous to the evolution of all mankind.

*"Education is the most powerful weapon
which you can use to change the world."*
—*Nelson Mandela*

How little did I understand how true that was until I was a victim of it.

You Are The One With The Power

There is a battle going on today for women to be seen as they truly are and respected for their skills, talents, abilities, and insight. It is a battle that we are slowly winning, and it is being done by courageous women who defy what they say is 'normal.'

In 1967, Kathrine Switzer made history when she defiantly became the first woman to officially run in the Boston Marathon.

As she ran, Jock Semple, a race official, jumped off the press bus and ran after her. "He grabbed me, threw me back and said, 'Get the hell out of my race and give me those numbers.'" Her boyfriend at the time intervened, pushing Semple away while Switzer continued running the race.

Her coach Arnie yelled, "Run like hell!"

Katherine told her coach, "I have to finish this race even if I have to finish it on my hands and my knees. Because if I don't finish the race, nobody is going to believe that women can do this. Nobody is going to believe that women should be here."

She did finish the race.

It was all caught in an iconic photograph that galvanized the women's movement and helped change the game for female athletes. "It changed everything," she said. "It changed my life and it changed millions of women's lives."

"My message to young girls is that you can do much more than you ever can imagine," Switzer said.

On The Basis of Sex

As a woman, there will be hard things that you will have to face to see your dreams and aspirations come true. The bigger your dream, the more you will have to fight for it. My time in the mental hospital against my will for telling the truth has made me more determined than ever to help you see your dream come true.

You are powerful and strong. Never let anyone tell you differently. You are as capable as anyone else on the planet and your hopes and goals just as valid. You dream as big as you can, and the dreamers will catch up with you to build it! You just run as fast as you can, and other runners will join you!

Don't let anyone ever tell you that you are crazy for having a humongous dream. Go for it everyday and you will get there, even if you end up in a mental hospital to do it. LOL.

> *"I ask no favor for my sex; all I ask of our brethren is that they take their feet off our necks."*
>
> *—Ruth Bader Ginsburg,*
> *the eminently quotable Supreme Court Justice*

By the way, can I share a secret with you? You can fight back against the system and win. That is what I am planning to do. I was incarcerated illegally, and they will be paying for that. You watch and see. Want to see how I am doing with that? Connect with me on Facebook at https://www.facebook.com/envyfactor/ and when justice is served you will hear all about it. You can also go to www.envyfactor.com where I share important documents that you can use if you have been unjustly hospitalized and may even prevent you from being taken against your will in the first place.

These last two chapters have been very serious but offered vital information to you for living the life of your dreams. They were hard for me to write but I knew that these stories had to be told. In chapter 10, we are going to lighten it up and I will share with you some great principles that will help you get to where you want to be faster.

CHAPTER 10

"NO Excuses on the Road to Success!

The real test is not whether you avoid this failure, because you won't. It's whether you let it harden or shame you into inaction, or whether you learn from it; whether you choose to persevere."

—Barack Obama

L OOKING AT SUCCESSFUL PEOPLE FROM the outside, it can seem like success is just a happy accident that you fall into at birth. Perhaps that may be true for some people, but lasting success happens by design. How do you create a successful life? You do it yourself every single day.

You must make intentional choices and commit to your vision.

I had a friend who believed that success in life was like a lottery. Everything in life came down to pure dumb luck as far as he was concerned. He saw that I had a house, and he didn't have a house. I had two cars, he only had one car. From his outside perspective, I had everything. He said to me, "You're just lucky because your father got you that job at Ford."

I got so angry at that remark! "My father didn't go to work or show up for any of my shifts for me. Anything that you see that I have, I had to go and put in the work for it, every single day. Yes, my father got me in the door at the company, but he never worked a day for me."

You must do the work. You start creating success the minute you commit to putting in the work. You must commit to spending the time, strength, and brainpower to get yourself to your goal. Your current situation may look nothing like your dream. Start thinking about it as I did in the foundry. Begin from the inside out and train yourself right where you are.

Keeping this commitment won't always be easy. There will be people that will help you and guide you along the way, but to be successful, you must be willing to be 100 % honest with yourself. Don't be tempted to make up reasons why you can't. Excuses sound best to those who are telling them. The next time you tell someone why you can't do anything, remember that is only a lie to make you feel like your choices are justified. Don't do it! When you make excuses to justify yourself, you may feel more comfortable, but it won't change everybody else knowing that it is only an excuse.

Be ready to stretch and grow as you pursue your success. You won't be able to stay the same and become successful. Goal-setting expert Jim Rohn recommends setting big goals so that you eventually grow into a person who can accomplish them. Don't settle for mediocre objectives that are too easy or safe. They won't give you true satisfaction when you accomplish them. You will need to learn and build new skills to hit the target you have set.

"Fall seven times, stand up eight."

—*Japanese Proverb*

You may be thinking, "But what if I fail?" Fail your ass off! If you get knocked down seven times, stand up eight. Be resilient and try again, using what you learned the first time to take you farther than before. Ultimately, every experience will polish you—*if you let it*. Anything can change.

Don't waste time feeling bad about yourself. Let's say your brother has a better job than you. Are you the loser of the family? Not if you say otherwise! Anything can change. Only you can decide if you are a loser. Others may not have a high opinion of your chances, but they are only spectators. You are the only player that matters! After college, you have roughly 80 years to "win" at your life. Change is your chance become more. Today is the best day to get started.

Change isn't always the monster under the bed. It is also the bird learning to fly, or the caterpillar that becomes a butterfly. Change is a catalyst for growth. Each obstacle that you face causes you to grow and become the person ready to handle more success. Understand that success will eat you alive if you are not ready for it. That's why so many "instant successes" don't stay that way: they are one hit wonders. They do not know how to handle the increased pressure and responsibilities that make up the leadership aspect of success. It will make you a leader, so you better get ready!

Nobody could walk through those foundry doors for me. It was something I had to do on my own. I had to walk through that hell of fire, molten iron, and dirt. No one else could walk that path and make me become the strong woman I am now. I had to live through that experience and had my commitment tested every day until I came out on the other side. Difficult, frightening experiences test us and make us stronger.

I lived through my tough times and they didn't break me. My life had been threatened more than once, but I couldn't retreat. Those horrible, horrible experiences gave me the strength I needed to go into business. I learned that *if I could live through those things, I can do anything.* It taught me that there was nothing else that could hold me back if I wanted it. I am unstoppable. I am bullet proof. I want you to learn that same powerful lesson: *you are stronger than you think.* There will be some tough times in your life that you don't want to go through, but you may have no other choice. Step up, lean in, and walk through your fire to the rewards on the other side.

These lessons are a part of the price of success. I pray that you never face the life-threatening situations I have lived through. Still, I want to prepare you for the fact that the road ahead has a few bumps on it. There will be setbacks that challenge you. People who disappoint you. As difficult as these experiences are, don't let your heart be swayed. Don't quit your dreams. The skills that bring you to success have their own rewards: resilience, work ethic, vision, and ambition. These rewards are worth so much more than the price of the hard lessons that experience teaches.

It's time to take a hard look at what staying the same for so long has done to you. Choosing to stay where you are comes at a steep price. Staying where you are keeps you in the role of victim. You are teaching your kids that they are victims, too. Being miserable and having your children see Mommy and Daddy are unhappy. Mommy and Daddy can't afford things. Mommy and Daddy can't do things, can't go places—staying stuck is selfish.

When you choose to stay broke and miserable, it is the most selfish thing that you could do to your children. It truly is. There is a price to success, true, but there is a greater cost to inertia. Choosing the status quo and living a meagre existence is selfish.

While you are sitting there thinking about how you are worried about the bills you can't pay this week, do you realize that you are going to be worried about the bills next week? You might as well step up and stop lying to yourself. You are better than that! Instead of making your children the excuse for not pursuing your dream, make your children your reason why you get up in the morning to pursue that dream. Get up and start being the victor of your life and for your family!

Turn it all around—and teach your kids what they are going to need to know, because one day, it will be their turn to build a life for their families. As I have said before, my father is no prince. Yet, he taught me to be scrappy, spirited, and tough. I learned my work ethic from him, and for those qualities, I am grateful.

Know this truth: You are going to work anyway. You would be a stay-at-home-mother anyway. Why not step up and build your dreams? That is the most beautiful thing that we are doing with this shopping annuity. It moves me so deeply. The money is there. It is a trillion-dollar business. Online shopping accounts for trillions and trillions of dollars in commerce because the money is there. If you work hard enough, it is there. It is also letting parents be parents. Home-based businesses are bringing back parental presence in the home. In time, our children are stronger, and in turn, our communities grow stronger. That is the power of living your dream.

There are a lot of kids in my neighborhood, only 18-19 years old, who are pregnant. I was thinking about it the other day, about the choices that led to these girls becoming mothers. I said to my friend, "You know why your daughter got pregnant? Because that boy had a car and she didn't. So, he was a hero." In her mind, that boy had the freedom she was craving, but it was an illusion.

My father bought me my first two cars and gave me a greater independence. A boy with a car couldn't be the hero to me, because I already had my own. There was still a price to that: I felt indebted to my father to have a better life. He bought me those two cars to build a sense of independence in me. He sacrificed his time working weekends and overtime to have the money to buy a teenage girl a $1,500 car.

This is how it came about. My father wanted to encourage my entrepreneurial spirit. When I was 15 years old, my father bought me a motorcycle for $300. It was a 1989 Honda Rebel motorcycle that needed a little tuning up. We spent weekends cleaning it up and getting it ready for me to ride.

After a week of cleaning up the motorcycle, my mother flipped out. She did not want me to ride a motorcycle. It was too dangerous. She wanted me to drive a car. So, we sold the motorcycle for $1,800 to my Aunt Susie, because my aunt wanted to learn to ride a motorcycle. What would be better than a Honda Rebel, a touring bike that was designed for female riders?

We sold it to her for $1,800, and we used that money to get me a Chevy Cavalier as my first car. It was a manual drive, five-speed. I chose a stick because he put an irresistible carrot in front of me. If I learned how to drive a stick, he would let me drive his Corvette.

My father made a point of teaching me business skills. He didn't just give me the car. He showed me this is how we will flip this motorcycle to make enough money to get you the car. That was a different kind of gift, in a sense. I am proud of the work I put in to get where I have.

The Secret of My Success—5 Principles To Live By

1. Goal Setting

If you were going to take a cross-country road trip, chances are you would have a destination in mind. You would gas up your car, pack clothes, and figure out the details, like eating and sleeping. Goal setting is the road map to your dreams. If you want to reach your goals, both you and your goals must be SMART.

S: Specific—Your goal should be clear and specific. "I want to lose weight" is unspecific. What counts as losing weight? Two or three pounds? Five pounds? "I want to lose twenty pounds" is a clear, specific amount.

M: Measurable—This goes hand in hand with being specific. Measuring tells you when you have reached your goal. "I want to make five phone calls this week" is easy to measure. Did you only make four?

Maybe circumstances made it impossible, maybe you were procrastinating—measuring helps you decide if your efforts are reasonable or not.

A: Actionable—You want it done? Write down what you are going to do, not what you are going to be. (Save that for your daily affirmations!) Example: "I will get to work at 8:45", not "I am going to show up earlier at work". Give yourself clear directions on what to do.

R: Realistic—This can be tricky to determine. How big is the change you are trying to make? "Getting signed to a record label in the next three months" is measurable, but probably unrealistic when all your vocal performances are taking place in the shower and your drive to work (sorry, carpool buddies)! Try "Performing at an open-mike by the end of the month". That goal would stretch you out of your comfort zone, but it is still easily achievable.

T: Timely—Every goal you make should have a date. Giving yourself a deadline is a big motivator. It is up to you to set a date that works for your life. You can revisit the due date and change it if circumstances have changed. For example, if your goal was to earn a master's degree, and you missed the window to apply for the current year's program, then it makes sense to change your goal date accordingly.

2. Master Mind

Andrew Carnegie, the world's first billionaire, attributed all his wealth to the mastermind principle. The principle is simple: two or more people gathered with their minds in harmony for the same creative purpose. Success requires cooperation.

This principle has one key element: picking the right people. If you are the smartest person in the room, you are in the wrong room. You may have an awesome idea, but if your five (wrong) people tell you it's junk, then you will be tempted to give up on your idea.

Finding the right people is actually two challenges in one. First, you have to give up people who aren't invested in your dream. There will be people in your life that you will outgrow. You love them still, but they are not going to grow. They are weeds in your garden. They won't be able to work in harmony towards your goal.

Challenge number two, you must find people who can align themselves with your vision. You may have to search out mastermind partners. There is meetup.com, where you can connect with like-minded people. Start scheduling mastermind events before you think are ready. Even if you only meet people who are awesome to be around, you win.

3. Mentor

A mentor or accountability partner is an important aspect of success. They share their experience, good and bad, to help guide you on your path. They have insight, can recommend the books that helped them grow or warn you away from mistakes that cost them on the journey to their goals.

4. Mirror Work

This is brain work. Reprogram your subconscious to be one of a person who can accomplish their goals. The most successful people are meticulous in their thoughts and their words.

Develop the attitude that every challenge is something that is polishing you. Take responsibility for your attitude and your response. This is a discipline that you will develop over time. You must persevere.

5. No "Wooden Nickels"

One of the most important lessons working in the foundry taught me is that life is too short to be chasing "wooden nickels." (From the expression, "Don't take any Wooden Nickels", meaning "don't get cheated.") Think about your job. If you don't love it, if it is not fulfilling your major purpose, then you are cheating yourself. You might make money, but it will be wooden nickels in the end. Go for your dreams.

CHAPTER 11

A Star Is Born

"Some women choose to follow men, and some women choose to follow their dreams. If you're wondering which way to go, remember that your career will never wake up and tell you that it doesn't love you anymore."

—Lady Gaga

Y OU CAN SEE THE UNIVERSE in one of two ways. Either everything is no big deal, or you are like a child, amazed at the wonder of everything around them. You cannot fully understand what you really are and made up of. It is no different than not understanding how a star is suspended in the sky and has enough power to shine bright enough for all the world to see it.

I am telling you, God Made YOU with that same wonder! In that same way beyond your imagination and He wants you to shine so bright for all the world to see. You were created for a reason and a purpose and it is your time to shine.

Tucker: The Man and His Dream

Karin loved her job at the bakery, but at some point every day, her stomach would be in knots. She was terrified that her secret would be out. Karin could not read. She would make up excuses to hide the fact that she struggled to multiply recipes. She couldn't write notes and had to rely on other staff to help her read the recipes because she "forgot her glasses at home."

Living with this secret was exhausting. Karin was tired of feeling uncertain and embarrassed. She dreamed of a day where she didn't have to hide or make excuses for her reading and math skills. She saw customers sitting in the bakery's café with newspapers and magazines. Karin wondered what it would feel like to want to read for pleasure. She secretly suspected that they weren't really reading but using the newspapers as props to look busy and avoid talking to people. Even if that was the case, Karin longed to sit and read one herself.

Everything came to a head one day when there was no one around to help her and she messed up an order big time. Thankfully, her boss liked her work ethic and didn't fire her but made it clear that this couldn't happen again. It was the wakeup call she needed.

Karin found out about literacy classes at the local community center and decided to take an assessment. She was paired up with Elinor, a retired kindergarten teacher who was patient and supportive. Karin's reading skills grew, and so did her confidence. Her employer noticed the change, and promoted her to the position of supervisor, a role where she wrote lists and tasks for 10 other employees. Now people were coming to Karin for help! It turned out that Karin was a patient teacher. Eventually, her boss put her in charge of training new people.

You may feel like your life doesn't hold a lot of promise right now. Maybe one wrong decision took you down a path where bad decisions began piling up until they snowballed. You feel like you were buried under an avalanche that you couldn't escape. Don't lose hope. Start looking for your dream.

When I started this journey, I was still a child in many ways. I felt powerless to make my own choices. Sometimes I let my father make my decisions for me. Other times, it just seemed like my life was a series of consequences falling like dominoes.

Today, I am living a life that I am designing for myself. I make enough money that I can travel and dress in a style I had dreamed about as a child. More importantly, I get to change other people's lives. Take some time today and think about what your life would look like if you began living your dream.

> *"Don't be afraid to be ambitious about your goals.*
> *Hard work never stops. Neither should your dreams."*
>
> —*Dwayne Johnson*

Your History is Not Your Future

We all struggle with pain from the past. Our mistakes (and sometimes the consequences of other peoples' mistakes) can seem to loom over our lives like black storm clouds on the horizon. When that happens, you need to stop and forgive yourself for being human. Yes, it happened, but you are not stuck! You do not have to repeat the choices that lead you to that place.

Your history does not define who you are or what you are capable of achieving. No matter where you grew up, or if your parents weren't there for you when you needed them, you are the one who gets to choose the labels you wear. Trade in the negative labels for the ones that match your dream.

Turn Struggle into Success

As you start working toward your dream, you may need to check your vision. I'm not talking about eyesight. I want you to get a clear vision of what you are working for. Make sure that you know what you want and start planning the steps to get there.

Look at the people who support your dream and the skills you currently have in your life and count them as your 'Advantages.' Take inventory of the obstacles you may face. (Yes, sometimes people are obstacles!)

Brainstorm strategies and solutions with the people in your mastermind group. They will come up with ideas that may surprise you. Your mastermind group will help you face your trials and turn them into triumphs by looking for new opportunities.

If you have absolutely nothing and wanted to turn your life around, GO TO THE LIBRARY! The library is a vault of endless inspiration, knowledge, and wisdom.

Knowledge is Power

Even though you may think that you know everything about your dream, don't stop learning. Read everything you can about business and keeping a growth mindset. Your goal is knowledge. Become like martial arts legend Bruce Lee, who said, "**Absorb what is useful, discard what is not, add what is uniquely your own.**"

Keep polishing yourself, and you will find new opportunities become available to you. Talk with your mentor and ask them what they found was the most helpful, the most useful knowledge that they have gained, and then study it deeply. Your confidence will grow as you perfect your abilities. Knowledge drives out fear.

Commit to Courage

My days in the foundry taught me that I could not just try it once and quit. Day after day, I would lace up my steel-toed boots and know that I would have to walk into hell one more time. I knew I would be working alongside difficult, dangerous men who could hurt me, but I persisted.

You will have to learn to "lace up" your own "steel toes" as you chase after your dream. There will be times when you want to stay home in bed and pull the blankets over your head. Instead, you are going to get prepared physically and mentally. Some women call makeup their "war-paint." Football fans paint their faces to cheer their team to victory. I like the image of getting ready for your day like you are preparing for battle. Fix your mindset. You must commit to courage.

Defeat the Dream Killers

Hopefully, you will not have life-threatening situations to deal with in your daily life. It is no joke. You do have enemies that you must battle: the people who laugh at your dreams and tell you that you don't have what it takes to succeed. These people drain your energy and your hope.

If you can, cut ties with these people completely. If that is not fully possible, reduce the time you spend around them. Do not let your vision be a topic for discussion with them. They may be surprised at first, but you are keeping your dream safe.

Become Bulletproof

Conquer your dream killers by listening to motivational speakers, like Jim Rohn, Zig Ziglar, and others. Go to conferences with leaders, like Jack Canfield and Raymond Aaron. You must invest in your mental health and your future wealth by growing strong in your vision and your conviction that you will succeed.

Daily reading, or daily listening, will help inoculate you from the poisonous words of dream killers. You are changing the soundtrack in your mind and it takes time. Train your mind to resist negative messages and it will become bulletproof

Money Changes Everything

I am giving you a "homework assignment": read Robert Kiyo-saki's *Rich Dad, Poor Dad* and *Cash Flow Quadrant.* Buy your own copies, because you are going to want to mark them up as you read them. One key point that Kiyosaki emphasizes is that you either have money working for you, or you are working for money. It's time to start making money work for you.

Research opportunities that are available through the internet and e-commerce. Look for ways to create multiple income streams.

Eventually, you will be able to automate your money, and see revenues coming from assets you have already created.

Oh, The Places You'll Go!

Try this exercise: pick up a pen and a piece of paper. Write out one thing you want to see happen in the next twelve months. It can be practical like "save $1,500", or it can be fun, like "take the family to Disneyland". It's up to you. Just write it down. Seriously.

Next, write down three to five steps you need to take to make your goal a reality. Grab a calendar and start plunking in those steps. Track your progress every week and remind yourself of the prize waiting at the finish line. Write down when you got further than you expected, and when you got your butt kicked. Both things will happen, and it's important to remember that you will have amazing days, especially when you are feeling down in the dumps. You can do it. Your success story starts here.

On Your Mark, Get Set...

You can do so much more than you realize, so much more than you think. Keep these words stuck on your bathroom mirror and on your refrigerator door. Write them on a piece of paper that you keep in your wallet to remind yourself that you are working for your dream.

Wherever you are in *your* journey, I wish you the strength to pursue your passion, the vision to focus on your dreams, and the courage to share your love and generosity with the world.

If you need help with your journey, I would consider it an honor to help and support you. My dream is to help others have their financial dreams come true. Contact me by going to berichyou.com or through Facebook ~RaNae Envy and let's see how we can work together.

CHAPTER 12

"If They Don't Give You A Seat At The Table, Bring A Folding Chair."

—Shirley Chisholm
First Black Woman Elected To The U.S. Congress

WHAT A JOURNEY THIS HAS been. I never knew that what I went through as a child and young adult would be put into a book. My messes have become messages and my tests have become testimonies.

My life has completely changed, and I couldn't be more thankful. Being told as a child that the only thing I am good for is to be married and have kids motivated me to want to become more. Not that I have a problem with any woman who feels that is her calling. It is a noble one. Where would we be without awesome moms who make the choice to stay at home and raise amazing kids? I knew that I was made for something different. My stars led in another direction.

I realized that part of my calling in life was to give people a choice in how their lives turn out. There is a war going on and it is all about control and who has it. There are two sides in this war. Massive world-wide online companies that want to suck you into buying from them while they destroy other companies. They don't care about the environment or people as long as they have the money and the control. On the other side are companies that want to empower not only their customers, but employees and sales teams, while helping those less fortunate. That is why I love Shop.com.

There is massive influence in our collective buying power! JR Ridinger is the owner of the only BIG company that thinks the way he does. You can have whatever you want as long as you help enough people get what they want. If our current funds are being spent to create new wealth kings, then it CAN and WILL create economic alchemy! Economic alchemy is changing one thing into another. JR has God given genius. He said in the beginning he wanted to get rich by helping others get what they want.

He talks a lot about his famous father, who was a well-respected Football High School coach. He was even in the Hall of Fame of High School Football coaches. JR said what his father would do is find the troubled kids or a kid not doing well, and take him under his wing to get them to believe in themselves. His belief in them was so great, they ended up going on to college and doing great things. JR embodies this. He says that you have to succeed for others to believe that they can succeed!

Change Your Life

My goal throughout this book has been to help you see that you can change your life. I want to take this last chance to summarize all the lessons I learned and want you to remember.

1. Your Past Never Defines Your Future

I had to let go of my past and the things that happened, so I could embrace a beautiful future.

2. No One Controls You

I spent a lot of my life letting others control who I am and what I do. That is no more. Now I make the decisions and I accept the consequences for them. It is such a free place to be.

3. Fear Is Never Your Friend

Have you ever heard what the acronym F.E.A.R means? False Evidence Appearing Real. That is what fear does. It shows you things that aren't real and uses them to convince you not to do the thing that you are supposed to do.

Fear and success are enemies. If you have one, then you don't have the other. Make the choice today to let fear go and instead replace it with . . .

4. Faith

Faith and success are best friends. Think of faith as the girlfriend who prejudges a guy and protects her friend from the bad ones. If you want to get to know success, then faith must become your friend first.

Another way of describing faith is belief. Even though you can't see it yet, you know it is there and it is possible. That belief for me also includes God. He is the one who strengthens me and empowers me to become the best me possible.

5. Opposition Will Happen

There are forces, both physical and spiritual, that don't want you to succeed. They will come against you and try to get you to stay little and mediocre.

Don't let them. You have the power to become more and reach your goals and dreams in life.

It Is Time

The Future is Female and LOVE! You can do anything, darling!

In the year of 2018, an American became a real-life Princess of The Royal family of the United Kingdom and the other Commonwealth realms!

Meghan, Duchess of Sussex, born Rachel Meghan Markle on August 4, 1981, is a retired American actress, who became a member of the British royal family upon her marriage to Prince Harry. She is the first American to marry into the British royal family since 1937.

Markle was born and raised in Los Angeles, California, and has a mixed ethnic heritage. She was married once before and divorced, which is unprecedented for a royal!

She is not only proof you can have anything you dream. She is also proof that TRUE LOVE can conquer all! She is proof that you truly can be the change you want to see.

In a 2015 speech at the UN International Women's Day, she recalled, "A pivotal moment reshaped my notion of what is possible!"

As a young 11-year-old girl, she and her classmates were asked to do a social studies assignment that involved paying attention to commercials and thinking about the message they are trying to convey.

Meghan noticed that the Ivory dishwasher soap commercial only targeted women. She didn't agree with that message and she put pen to paper to spark a real change.

She wrote a letter to Procter & Gamble (Ivory soap's manufacturer), powerhouse American women's rights attorney Gloria Allred, then-first lady Hilary Clinton, and Nick News anchor Linda Ellerbee.

In the letter, she encouraged Ivory soap to change the message because she felt moms shouldn't be tasked with doing all the chores.

She suggested they change the line to, "People all over America are fighting greasy pots and pans." Changing the phrase from "women" to "people."

Due to the power of the pen, Ivory soap changed the commercial to include Meghan's suggestion of the word "people" instead of only "women."

RaNae Envy

In her life, Meghan accredited her father for giving her the courage to stand up for what she believes in. In that speech she said, "He encouraged me to write letters, so I did—to the most powerful people I could think of."

We teach our kids they are powerful beyond measure and we want them to accomplish more than we ever could. That's the beauty of the circle of life. Going as far as one can go in your lifetime, is your gift to leave for the next generation.

I want to encourage you that now is the time. We never know how much time we have left on this earth. Tomorrow is not guaranteed. If you are going to take action, then the only time is NOW.

When you see your dreams become reality, it is the most wonderful thing you will ever experience.

On Facebook today as I write this, I posted, "I had a crazy dream, woke up & realized it was my life. Then I paused and was so grateful for this crazy, amazing life."

In the end, it is not so much about conquering the world. It's about not letting the world conquer you!

Go back through this book and mark the chapters that speak to you the most. These are the best places for you to start. Act on what you have learned, and you will see your life change.

As I go, I want to leave you with my favourite quote. Let it brighten your day as it always brightens mine.

"Our deepest fear is not that we are inadequate. Our deepest fear is that we are powerful beyond measure. It is our light, not our darkness that most frightens us. We ask ourselves, Who am I to be brilliant, gorgeous, talented, fabulous? Actually, who are you not to be? You are a child of God. Your playing small does not serve the world. There is nothing enlightened about shrinking so that other people won't feel insecure around you. We are all meant to shine, as children do. We were born to make manifest the glory of God that is within us. It's not just in some of us; it's in everyone. And as we let our own light shine, we unconsciously give other people permission to do the same. As we are liberated from our own fear, our presence automatically liberates others."

Marianne Williamson is from her book, A Return To Love: Reflections on the Principles of A Course in Miracles

To A Life Worth Living,

RaNae Envy
Author, Visionary, Entrepreneur, Business Consultant

RICH
\ 'rich \
adjective

Definition of rich

1: having abundant possessions and especially material wealth

2: a) having high value or quality

b) well supplied or endowed a city rich in traditions

3: magnificently impressive: SUMPTUOUS

4: a) vivid and deep in color a rich red

b) full and mellow in tone and quality a rich voice

c) having a strong fragrance rich perfumes

5: highly productive or remunerative a rich mine

6: a) having abundant plant nutrients rich soil

b) highly seasoned, fatty, oily, or sweet rich foods

c) high in the combustible component a rich fuel mixture

d) high in some component cholesterol-rich foods

7: a) ENTERTAINING also: LAUGHABLE

b) MEANINGFUL, SIGNIFICANT rich allusions

c) LUSH rich meadows

8: pure or nearly pure rich lime

It appears that according to Merriam-Webster, I am RICH on all levels, by all accounts, and by all definitions. All 8 to be exact. Review each definition of what it means to be RICH and think about having all levels in your life. How rich are you when you really think about it? I'd bet that many of you out there are richer than you think!

Mir•a•cle

/'mirək(ə)l/

noun

- a surprising and welcome event that is not explicable by natural or scientific laws and is therefore considered to be the work of a divine agency: "the miracle of rising from the grave" *synonyms*: supernatural phenomenon, mystery, prodigy, sign

- a highly improbable or extraordinary event, development, or accomplishment that brings very welcome consequences: "it was a miracle that more people hadn't been killed or injured"

- an amazing product or achievement, or an outstanding example of something: "a machine which was a miracle of design" *synonyms*: wonder, marvel, sensation, phenomenon, astonishing feat, amazing achievement